CARRIER BATTLE IN THE PHILIPPINE SEA

THE MARIANAS TURKEY SHOOT
JUNE 19-20, 1944

By

BARRETT TILLMAN

PHALANX
Publishing Co., Ltd.
1051 Marie Avenue
St. Paul, MN 55118 U.S.A.
612/454-0607

ISBN: 1-883809-04-5

Written by Barrett Tillman

Illustrations by John C. Valo

Map by Steven Carley

Published by:

Phalanx Publishing Co., Ltd.
1051 Marie Avenue West
St. Paul, MN 55118-4131 USA

Printed in the United States of America

GLOSSARY OF U.S. AIRCRAFT

TYPE	MANUFACTURER	DESIGNATION	NAME
Fighter	Grumman	F6F	Hellcat
Fighter	Vought	F4U	Corsair
Fighter	Eastern Aircraft	FM-2	Wildcat**
Dive bomber	Douglas	SBD	Dauntless
Dive bomber	Curtiss	SB2C	Helldiver
Torpedo bomber	Grumman	TBF	Avenger
Torpedo bomber	Eastern Aircraft	TBM	Avenger*

* The same Grumman Avenger license-built.
** The same Grumman Wildcat lilcense built.

GLOSSARY OF JAPANESE AIRCRAFT

TYPE	MANUFACTURER	DESIGNATION	NAME
Fighter	Mitsubishi	A6M	Zero, Zeke
Twin-engine night fighter	Nakajima	J1N1	Irving
Dive bomber	Aichi	D3A	Val
Dive bomber	Yokosuka	D4Y	Judy
Torpedo bomber	Nakajima	B5N	Kate
Torpedo bomber	Nakajima	B6N	Jill
Twin-engine bomber	Mitsubishi	G4M	Betty
Twin-engine bomber	Yokosuka	P1Y	Frances
Twin-engine transport	Yokosuka	L2D	Tabby*
Float-reconnaissance	Aichi	E13A	Jake
Reconnaissance	Nakajima	C6N1	Myrt

*A Douglas DC-3 license built.

ADDITIONAL GLOSSARY

AMM:	Aviation machinist mate
AOM:	Aviation ordnanceman
ARM:	Aviation radioman
BB:	Battleship
CA:	Cruiser
CAG:	Air group commander
CIC:	Combat information center
CTF:	Commander (of) task force
CV:	Fleet aircraft carrier
CVE:	Escort aircraft carrier
CVG:	Carrier air group
CVL:	Light aircraft carrier
DD:	Destroyer
ECM:	Electronic countermeasures
FDO:	Fighter direction officer
LSO:	Landing signal officer
TF:	Task force
TG:	Task group
UHF:	Ultra–high frequency
VHF:	Very–high frequency
VB:	Bombing squadron
VF:	Fighting squadron
VT:	Torpedo squadron

PARTICIPANTS

Ranks are as of June 1944

Lt. Zenji Abe, Air Group 652, Junyo
Lt. Cdr. Fred A. Bardshar, CAG–27, Princeton
Lt. Harold L. Buell, VB–2, Hornet
Lt(jg) George Bush, VT–51, San Jacinto
ARM1/c David Cawley, VB–10, Enterprise
Lt. Cdr. Gerald R. Ford, Monterey
Lt. Donald Gordon, VF–10, Enterprise
Cdr. David McCampbell, CAG–15, Essex
Lt(jg) Richard B. Morland, fighter director, Lexington
Lt(jg) Warren R. Omark, VT–24, Belleau Wood
Lt Cdr. James D. Ramage, VB–10, Enterprise
AOM2/c Allen J. Rogers, VT–28, Monterey
Lt. Richard Stambook, VF–27, Princeton
Lt(jg) Benjamin C. Tate, VT–24, Belleau Wood
Lt. Alex Vraciu, VF–16, Lexington
Ens. Wilbur B. Webb, VF–2, Hornet
Ens. Edward G. Wendorf, VF–16, Lexington

Special thanks to Capt. Akikhiko Yoshida, JMSDF (Retired), James F. Lansdale and James C. Sawruk and The Naval Institute Press for detailed information.

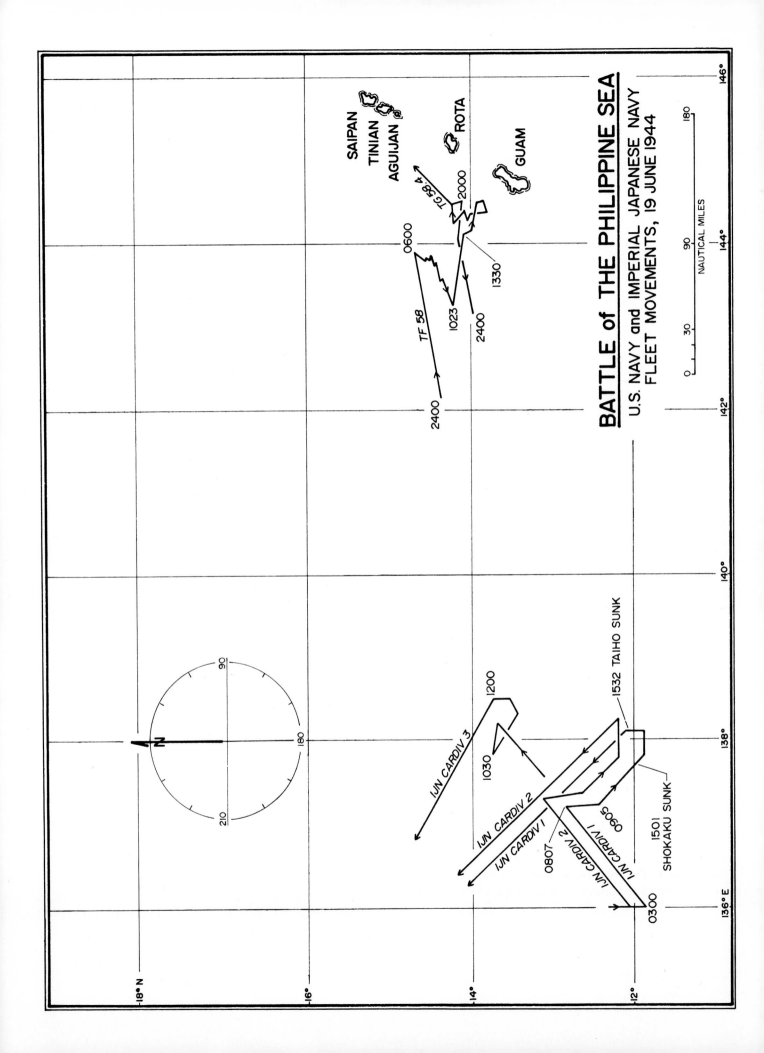

BATTLE of THE PHILIPPINE SEA

U.S. NAVY and IMPERIAL JAPANESE NAVY
FLEET MOVEMENTS, 19 JUNE 1944

NAUTICAL MILES

0   30   90   180

SAIPAN
TINIAN
AGUIJAN

ROTA

GUAM

TG 58 4
2000
1330

TF 58
0600
1023
2400
2400

N
90
180
210

IJN CARDIV 3
1200
1030
IJN CARDIV 2
IJN CARDIV 1
0807
IJN CARDIV 2
IJN CARDIV 1
0300
0905
1501
SHOKAKU SUNK
1532 TAIHO SUNK

18° N
16°
14°
12°

136° E   138°   140°   142°   144°   146°

PREFACE

West of the Mariana Islands in June 1944, the American and Japanese navies clashed in the greatest aircraft carrier battle of all time. Twenty-four flattops embarking 1,350 airplanes were directly engaged, excluding U.S. escort carriers and Japanese land-based units. Nothing remotely comparable will ever happen again.

In this, the 50th anniversary year of that event, the CV retains its geo-strategic importance. However, the carrier's vast quantity of half a century ago has diminished to the point where, in 1994, only some fifteen conventional flattops--operating tailhook airplanes--remain active in the U.S. and French navies. Those still owned by Argentina and Russia may never sail again.

Carriers will only become rarer on the world's oceans. Since 1916 some 250 conventional CVs have been commissioned--86% of them by the end of 1945. Flying from aircraft carriers is almost certainly the most difficult task that humans have routinely performed. And so esoteric is the carrier art that only four navies have conquered the enormous design, production and economic challenges to put those ships to sea. Britain, America, Japan and France all accomplished the feat with indigenous efforts, while the last-minute Soviet attempt virtually died aborning. The German and Italian navies never completed their carriers during WW II. A half-dozen other nations have employed U.S.- or British-built carriers for various times since then.

Today, only three of the Mariana combatants remain: USS *Yorktown* (CV-10), permanently moored at Charleston, South Carolina; *Hornet* (CV-12) mothballed in Bremerton, Washington; and USS *Cabot* (CVL-28) preserved in New Orleans, Louisiana. The last of their Japanese counterparts were broken up for scrap in 1947.

Surviving examples of WW II carrier aircraft are similarly rare. The star of the battle, the Grumman F6F Hellcat, is represented by some flying examples, as is the TBF/TBM Avenger. Far less numerous are SBD Dauntlesses and SB2C Helldivers. Of the Japanese aircraft involved, perhaps three Mitsubishi Zeros are flown anywhere in the world.

But ships and airplanes are easier to tabulate than the men who served and flew them. Every week--perhaps every day--another veteran of Task Force 58 or the First Mobile Fleet slips away, taking with him unforgettable experiences and irreplaceable knowledge, leaving an unfillable void.

The contributors to this reprise are long retired now. Most are grandparents; some are great-grandparents. None still fly, and few even sail. Occasionally they meet to discuss the events of their youth or to share those events with carrier aviators of another generation--young men and women who will never know the fear and frustration and loneliness of aerial combat; of massed navies fighting for control of the Pacific Ocean; of burning, sinking ships. Of empires won and lost.

When they are gone, we will never see their like again.

The following text is derived from a variety of primary and secondary sources, a few of which are contradictory. Any errors of interpretation on those points are mine.

Hull numbers of U.S. Navy ships are included, with the exception of aircraft carriers, which are listed separately in the appendices. Imperial Japan had no such system, though the U.S. Navy assigned hull numbers to enemy warships for intelligence purposes. The Japanese prefix HMIJS (His Majesty's Imperial Japanese Ship) is employed properly here--more so than the anglicized IJNS (Imperial Japanese Navy Ship) which I have used elsewhere.

The appendix contains a near-complete list of all Japanese carrier captains and senior squadron (*hikotai*) leaders engaged in the Battle of the Philippine Sea. To my knowledge, none of this data has ever appeared in English. Additionally, air group commanders (*kokutaicho*) and their subordinates are delineated for the first time, thus correcting previous publications.

Barrett Tillman

May 1994

6

The fast carrier, *Yorktown*, CV-10, departs Pearl Harbor on May 28, 1944 enroute to support the invasion of the Marianas and engage the Japanese fleet in the First Battle of the Philippine Sea. (National Archives)

Cabot, CVL-28, was one of the light carriers that made up Task Force 58, shown here in 1945. (R.M. Hill)

OPPONENTS

The Americans called it Operation FORAGER: reoccupation of the Mariana Islands. Japan's reposte was designated A-Go: the long-anticipated defense of those critically-important parts of the Empire. Partly seized from Germany in 1914, with the balance taken from U.S. control in December 1941, the mid-Pacific island chain screamed for attention by early 1944. The primary islands--Guam, Tinian and Saipan--afforded bases for land-based bombers that could attack Japan itself, 1,500 miles to the north.

And so the word went down: from the Joint Chiefs of Staff in Washington to Adm. Chester Nimitz at CinCPac in Hawaii to Adm. Raymond Spruance's Fifth Fleet. Marine Corps and Army troops were assigned, planning was completed, the logistics and shipping were provided, and the stage was set.

Task Force 58 had a depth of individual and corporate experience. Its commander, Vice Adm. Marc Mitscher, was only the 33rd naval officer designated an aviator and had previous combat commands both afloat and ashore. Three of his four task-group commanders were also long-time fliers, averaging 22 years in aviation: the super-aggressive J.J. Clark (TG-58.1); petulant A.E. Montgomery (58.2) and gentlemanly W.K. Harrill (58.4). Rear Adm. J.W. Reeves (58.3), a late-comer to air, had won his wings in 1936 but was both aggressive and capable.

Mitscher's four carrier groups were directly supported by a total of seven cruisers and 53 destroyers, plus Vice Adm. Willis Lee's force of seven fast battlewagons with cruisers and destroyers of his own. Since no surface threat arose, these 84 warships contributed additional radar coverage and massive antiaircraft gunfire to fleet defense.

Nearly three-quarters of the air group commanders (CAGs) and squadron leaders were Annapolis graduates. Three of the 15 air groups had prior combat tours and six had been in the Pacific more than six months. The senior air group was CVG-10, back in United States Ship *Enterprise* after a 1942-43 deployment. Ironically, she had the junior fighter skipper, Lt. R.W. Schumann out of the Annapolis class of '39. All other TF58 fighter leaders were lieutenant commanders or commanders, mostly of 1933-34 vintage.

One of them was Cdr. Paul Buie, whose "Airdales" had the greatest continuous experience. Fighting 16 had been aboard *Lexington* nine months and boasted a half-dozen aces so far, including the CO and a transfer from VF-6: Lt(jg) Alexander Vraciu. His tally of 12 was tops in TF-58, and about to increase dramatically.

Almost exclusively, Mitscher's squadrons flew new-generation carrier aircraft that had entered the fleet since Pearl Harbor. The Curtiss SB2C Helldiver had replaced the Douglas SBD Dauntless in all but two TF58 bombing squadrons while Grumman's TBF Avenger was the torpedo plane on both CVs and CVLs. The 10,000-ton

Vice Adm. Marc A. Mitscher (Chas. Kerlee via R.L. Lawson)

By June all of TF58's CV and CVL aircraft carriers were equipped with Grumman F6F-3s like this *San Jacinto* VF-51 Hellcat. (R.M. Hill)

Independence-class ships, far smaller than their 27,000-ton *Essex* team-mates, carried a 24-plane fighter squadron and nine TBFs.

Additionally, the "Iron Works" produced the standard carrier fighter, the superb F6F-3 Hellcat. Capable of 375 mph and propelled by a reliable 2,000-hp engine, the Hellcat was armed with six M2 .50 cal. machine guns with 2,400 rounds. Initiated to combat the previous September, it was now the dominant fighter in the Pacific. And, as of 18 June, it was flown by experienced, accomplished fighter pilots--including 15 aces in seven of Mitscher's squadrons.

Additionally, eight escort carriers (CVEs) were assigned to the Saipan landings under Rear Admirals G.F. Bogan and H.B. Sallada. They provided 193 FM-2 Wildcats and TBM-1 Avengers for close air support of the assault troops. Three additional CVEs embarked P-47D Thunderbolts of the Seventh Air Force's 318th Fighter Group, which would fly off the baby flattops once Saipan was secure. Two squadrons launched from *Manila Bay* and *Natoma Bay* on 23 June with the last "Jugs" flown ashore from *Sargent Bay* on 18 July.

On paper, at least, Admiral Jisabuo Ozawa's First Mobile Fleet (*Dai-ichi Kido Kantai*) looked impressive--nine carriers supported by five battleships, nine cruisers and 23 destroyers in

Vice Admiral Jisaburo Ozawa commanded the Japanese Mobile Fleet June 1944. (U.S. Naval Inst.)

addition to an oiler group. Greatest of the combatants was HMIJS *Taiho*, the largest carrier afloat except for USS *Saratoga*.

With 439 carrier fighters or bombers, plus 43 reconnaissance floatplanes, Ozawa hoped to even

D4Y1 Judy carrier bombers enroute to target. This aircraft was the Japanese Navy's only in-line engined service aircraft and carried its bombs internally. Later models were radial engined. (Donald Thorpe via J.F. Lansdale)

the odds with elements of eight naval air groups ashore in the Marianas. And help was needed. The Mobile Fleet embarked a mixture of old and new aircraft: 150 A6M5 (Zero) fighters and 84 A6M2 fighter-bombers; 119 D4Y3 (Judy) and D3A1 (Val) dive-bombers plus nine Judy scouts; and 86 B6N2 (Jill) and B5N2 (Kate) torpedo planes. Therefore, discounting all the Zeros and the speedy scouts, fewer than half of Ozawa's embarked aircraft possessed a genuine strike capability.

However, there were greater problems with experienced leadership. Ozawa was not an aviator, nor had he ever conducted a sea battle, but he wore a second hat as Commander Carrier Division One.

B6N2 Jill attack aircraft belonging to the 312 Hikotai of the 601st Kokutai. Photo was taken while unit was undergoing training. Diagonal stripe is indicative of the attack unit's leader. (Juzo Nakamura via J.F. Lansdale)

His other division commanders were Rear Adm. Takaji Joshima (CarDiv Two) and Sueyo Obayashi (CarDiv Three)--both former carrier captains but neither had actually fought at sea.

Though a few formation leaders were old hands, the overall experience level was barely equal to U.S. Navy advanced-training squadrons. The Zero fighter-bomber pilots, for instance, were restricted to glide-bombing because in training some had dived into the water with target fixation. Additionally, the Japanese had no equivalent of the U.S. Navy's well-proven air group commander (CAG) concept. Each *kokutai* had a commander--the air officer of the carrier division's flagship--responsible for administration of the embarked air groups in each CarDiv. But mission leaders were senior squadron COs who, despite some notable exceptions, tended to be less experienced than their American counterparts.

In truth, Ozawa was triple-damned, facing greater numbers of better trained and more experienced opponents with superior equipment. Ironically, such a condition had not existed prior to a major battle since Japan defeated Czarist Russia in Tsushima Strait in 1905--when the airplane was 18 months old.

The stage was set not only for the greatest aircraft carrier battle in history, but probably the greatest aerial battle as well. When the sun set on 19 June, TF58 had established the American record for most aerial victories claimed in one day: 380. To put that in perspective, naval aviators had (erroneously) claimed more than 100 kills just once before--during the Rabaul, New Britain strike of 11 November 1943. In comparison, the Marine Corps' best day of the war was 87 shootdowns; the top Army Air Force one-day tally against Japan was 66; and the best air-air score by 8th and 9th Air Force fighters in Europe was 174. Undeniably, all these figures were subject to normal exaggeration, but they do indicate the relative scale of each conflict.

PRELIMINARIES

Both sides knew that a fight was coming. In fact, en route to the Marianas, one of Mitscher's operations officers made good use of advance intelligence to lay a $1,000 bet: a fleet engagement before 20 June. Cdr. Gus Widhelm--a gifted aviator and night-fighter pioneer--was onto a good thing. When TF58 launched preparatory air strikes on 11 June, the Hellcats claimed nearly 100 kills--mainly over Saipan and Tinian. Their presence was a calling card that Tokyo could not ignore.

D4Y1-C reconnaissance version of Judy carrier bomber. 01-065 belonged to Hikotai T.101 of the 151st Kokutai, here pictured shortly before transferring to Harushima Island (Moen, Truk Is). From Truk Hikotai T.101 flew recon missions to the Marianas. (National Archives via J.F. Lansdale)

By June 1944 new Curtiss Helldivers had replaced most Douglas SBD aircraft as the Navy's dive-bombing workhorse. Largest dive-bomber squadron in TF 58 was LCDR J. W. Runyan's VB-1 with 40 SB2C-1s aboard *Yorktown*. (Author's coll.)

Two days later Imperial Japan reacted as Nimitz expected. Vice Adm. Ozawa's Mobile Fleet raised anchor at Tawi Tawi, Borneo and sortied, but too late to prevent the Fifth Amphibious Corps from going ashore on Saipan the 15th.

That same day Clark and Harrill's fighter pilots waged a hard-fought battle at Iwo Jima, chasing bandits in and out of poor weather. But the F6Fs succeeded in short-stopping Japanese aerial reinforcements southward to the Marianas. Then the two task groups steamed back to rejoin Mitscher. The time had come.

Whatever hope Ozawa may have entertained of surprising Spruance was dashed from the start. Operating in seven patrol areas, 28 American submarines were deployed from Ulithi to the Philippines and beyond. One of four boats hunting off Tawi Tawi was USS *Redfin* (SS-272) under Cdr. M.H. Austin, who had recently sunk two tankers in the area. He spotted the van of Ozawa's force leaving the anchorage and, though unable to attack, soon saw most of the remainder sortie as

well. That evening Austin surfaced and radioed a crucial contact report; Spruance and Mitscher now knew when to expect company.

Still, there was no option for the Imperial Navy or the Tojo cabinet. Aside from the Marianas' strategic importance, the islands were considered Japanese soil, as were Formosa and Korea. Tokyo had to fight.

A Douglas Dauntless SBD-5 from *Lexington*'s VB-16 between Saipan and Tinian on 15 June 1944. Only two squadrons of the venerable Dauntless remained with TF58 by this point in the war. (National Archives)

An SBD-5 of VB-10 shows off its distinctive perforated dive brakes as it rolls away from the photo plane. The Dauntless had excellent aileron response, allowing it to get on target in a dive much faster than other contemporary dive bombers. (USN via R.M. Hill)

19 JUNE 1944 – THE CLASH

Dawn broke at 0542 on Monday the 19th, revealing 3/10 cloud cover. Four hours later the two fleets steamed under a near-cloudless sky, marred only by contrails and smoke plumes. A 10 to 14-knot breeze remained easterly throughout the day, favoring the Japanese carriers which could advance on TF58 without turning away from the wind. It was perfect flying weather: unlimited visibility for bombers hunting ships--and for interceptors seeking bombers. Combined with the argus eye of radar, the meteorological conditions insured frequent and early contact with inbound raiders.

Owing to previous scouting reports, Ozawa had a good idea where to look for Mitscher, some 150 miles west of Saipan. Consequently, CarDiv Three began launching a 64-plane strike from CVLs *Chitose*, *Chiyoda* and *Zuiho* at 0830, two-thirds of which were Zero fighter-bombers. He followed with his main punch a half-hour later: 128 planes of

CarDiv One from *Taiho*, *Shokaku* and *Zuikaku*. The latter pair, sister ships, were veterans of Coral Sea, Eastern Solomons and Santa Cruz. In TF58, only *Enterprise* had ever fought enemy carriers.

The day began well for Mitscher's CVLs. At 0547 two *Monterey* Hellcats bounced a Judy 30 miles west of the task force as Lt(jg) W.T. Fitzpatrick and Ens. R.P. Granger of VF-28 split the morning's first kill. About the same time several Zekes attacked the two picket destroyers west of the battleships, *Stockham* (DD-683) and *Yarnall* (DD-541). The land-based fighters dropped light bombs, losing one of their number to *Yarnall's* gunners, and withdrew. Sailors and fliers alike wondered why the Japanese had circumvented 110 other American ships covering 360 square miles just to attack two "small boys."

Sporadic combats then spread eastward over the next hour or more, with *Belleau Wood's* VF-24 claiming three Zekes over Guam.

An F6F of VF-16 prepares to launch from *Lexington*. A heavy cruiser keeps pace in the distance. (National Archives)

Helldivers of LCDR J.D. Arbes' VB-8 prepare to take off from *Bunker Hill*. (Author coll. via R.M. Hill)

Meanwhile, the escort carriers were active during the morning as *Corregidor* Wildcats splashed two Zekes southeast of Tinian and a *Gambier Bay* section bagged a lone Kate over the island.

THE SEARCHERS

Three-plane search teams--usually two SB2Cs or TBFs escorted by an F6F--were launched about 0530. One of *Lexington's* escort pilots was Ens. E.G. Wendorf, who explained:

"This was strictly a 'volunteer' mission, and I think it was a great tribute to Air Group 16 that enough pilots and crews 'volunteered' that no one

had to be *ordered* to go. There were some doubts, however, by some of the 'volunteers' as to how their names became listed on the blackboard! Also, at the time we volunteered for the search mission, we were completely unaware of the events that were to transpire later in the day.

"The F6Fs each had two 500-pound armor-piercing bombs and the TBFs were armed with torpedoes. Our orders were that if we sighted the (Japanese) fleet, we were to concentrate on a low-level attack on one of the carriers in an attempt to damage it, giving our forces time to pursue.

"Fortunately for us, we only ran into their long-range scouts, for had we sighted the Japanese

Torpron One launches Avengers during Operation FORAGER as "Coal 82" gets the go signal on *Yorktown*'s deck. (Author's coll.)

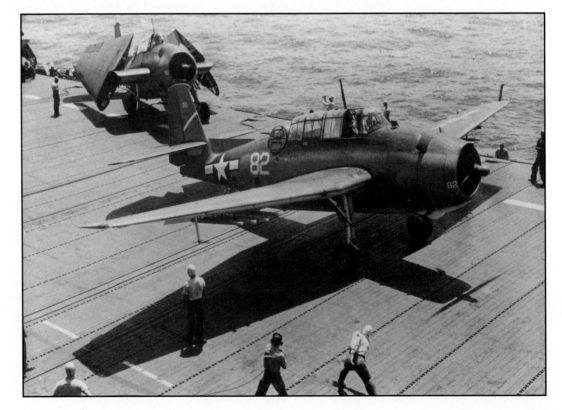

fleet, I'm sure it would have been a suicidal mission for us. The odds of three planes surviving an attack on an entire fleet--even with their diminished capacities and capabilities--I'm sure would have been extremely long!"

Scouting to 315 miles, the searchers then made a 75-mile cross leg before turning for home. At 0655 a *Yorktown* team was 200 miles west of the task force when the F6F pilot spotted a floatplane. Investigating, he identified it as a Jake and shot it down. Several minutes later two *Lexington* teams farther south and east did likewise. Ens. Wendorf bagged a Jill while another VF-16 pilot, Ens. W.H. Albert, splashed two. Obviously, Ozawa was probing for Mitscher.

Over the next 90 minutes, the searchers claimed nine more victims, as far as 310 miles out. The latter was another Jake, splashed by *Yorktown's* Lt. L.F. Clark, as Japanese doctrine remained unchanged from Midway: employ floatplanes for reconnaissance to preserve more carrier planes for attack.

In the hour between 0830 and 0940 an *Essex* team--Lt(jg) Clifford Jordan in an SB2C and Ens. James D. Bare in an F6F--splashed two Kates and a Jake as the Japanese continued probing.

Many scouts returned to TF58 during enemy air strikes. Wendorf found himself in that situation, recalling:

"As we approached our task group it was experiencing an attack, so they vectored the search teams to the unengaged side and held us while they repelled the attack. By the time we recovered aboard the Lex, we had been airborne pretty close

to seven hours and 45 minutes--a damn long time in a single-seat aircraft! This was possible only because we had weaved over the TBFs with a fixed power setting of about 1,500 rpm and 20-21 inches of manifold pressure for most of the search. Due to the extended length of our flight, we were not permitted to fly again that day."

In the afternoon two Judys ran afoul of VB-14 as six Helldiver pilots claimed a destroyed and a damaged 30 miles west of TG58.2. Finally, at 1620 a *Wasp* team split a Betty well south of Guam, probably northbound from the Marshalls.

Though these scouts missed most of the day's excitement, their contribution was important. Three hundred saltwater miles from one's ship, the most reliable engine can run in "automatic rough" even to the experienced ear. That experience cannot be appreciated by anyone who has never flown beyond sight of land in a single-engine aircraft.

"HEY, RUBE!"

From about 0700 the Hellcats were increasingly engaged. Concerned that the Japanese were funnelling land-based planes north from the Carolines, TF58 directed 33 F6Fs from VF-1, -2, -8, -15, -24 and -31 to Guam, where they claimed 30 Zekes and five bombers or attack planes. However, the carrier aviators had their hands full with additional enemy aircraft still on the ground and more taking off. Mitscher concluded that his force "was probably due for a working-over by both land-based and carrier-based planes."

G4M2 Model 22 Betty bomber under attack. This aircraft probably belonged to Hikotai K.601 attached to the 761st Kokutai which took part in the battle for the Marianas. The original negative shows the numerals 01-322 on the tail. (National Archives via J.F. Lansdale)

Less than a century before, captains preparing to engage the enemy promptly cleared their decks for action, and it was not significantly different with aircraft carriers. Mitscher ordered most of his on-deck bombers and torpedo planes launched as the quickest way of freeing deck space for much-needed fighters. One of *San Jacinto's* TBM pilots orbiting near the task force on sub CAP was 20-year-old Lt(jg) George Bush, who recalls: "After having made a water landing because of power failure, I was rescued by the destroyer *Clarence K. Bronson* (DD-668), and sat out the action with its crew."

Fighter pilots had no such inactivity. Shortly before 1000 Lt. Joseph Eggert in *Lexington's* CIC broadcast the old circus call, "Hey, Rube!" It meant for everyone to come running and lend a hand--which is precisely what CTF58 needed. One of Vice Adm. Lee's radars spotted a large formation more than 100 miles west, at 20,000 feet.

Curiously, the hostiles failed to close the task force promptly. Radar operators plotted the raid orbiting, and shortly they knew why. Mitscher's Japanese-language officer monitored the enemy airborne commander giving tactical data to his squadrons. This was almost certainly Lt. Cdr. Akira Tarui, the strike leader of CarDivOne. The time lost and secrecy squandered proved fatal. The big-deck carriers typically had 12 or 16 fighter pilots continuously briefed, sitting Condition Three alert in their ready rooms, ready to launch at ten-minute notice. During the delay TF58 began launching 140 F6Fs, bringing the airborne CAP to nearly 200 Grummans.

Lt. (jg) George Bush, a member of VT-51 in the First Battle of the Philippine Sea, was forced to ditch his depth charge laden Grumman Avenger because of engine failure. The future President of the United States and his two crewmen were rescued by a destroyer. (Bush Family via U.S. Naval Inst.)

RAID I

The first Japanese strike--identified as such by TF58 CIC teams--comprised 64 planes from CarDiv Three: Zekes and Jills. They finally got straightened out and closed the American fleet.

They found three of Mitscher's task groups (58.1, .3 and .2) arrayed north to south, respectively, with 58.4 west of 58.1, each 12 miles apart. Lee's battleships, 58.7, were 15 miles west of 58.3, thus forming the rough image of a reversed letter F.

A pair of F6F-3 Hellcats of VF-51, *San Jacinto*. The nearest aircraft is named "Little Joe". (National Archives via U.S. Naval Inst.)

CAG 15 skipper Dave McCampbell in his F6F "The Minsi" prepares to take off from *Essex.* (National Archives)

The disposition had a purpose. It reduced the necessity of overflying other task groups in the normal conduct of air operations, yet afforded mutual support both for radar coverage and fleet defense. A *Lexington* CIC officer, Lt(jg) Richard Morland, summed up the first intercept and all others that followed when he said, "The day was so clear that all we had to do was give the fighters a heading and they did the rest."

First on the scene were eight *Essex* F6Fs, led by VF-15's Cdr. C.W. Brewer. He made visual contact at 1035, still more than 50 miles from the force, and attacked from a 6,000-foot altitude advantage.

Brewer called out Zekes and Judys, but if his recognition was marginal, his aim was not. In minutes he and his wingman, Ens. R.L. Fowler, splashed four apiece. But even their hot pace was bettered by Lt(jg) G.R. Carr, who shot five torpedo planes out of formation. By the time reinforcements arrived, "Fabled Fifteen" had claimed 20 kills.

Elements of seven more squadrons piled in during the next half hour, shredding Air Group 653's ranks. Close behind Brewer and company was Cdr. Bill Dean's Fighting Two, whose eight Hellcats claimed nine Zekes and three Jills that broke off from the main formation. The *Hornet* pilots found they could not stay with the speedy Jills in a highspeed descent, though two *Cowpens* divisions (eight F6Fs) tried.

Other CVL squadrons conducted most of the remaining execution as VF-25, -27, -28 and -31 mauled the Japanese for some 20 miles. The shark-mouthed *Princeton* Hellcats were dominant in this phase of the battle, though two pilots were killed. CAG-27, Lt. Cdr. E.W.Wood, was lost when his empennage failed during a steep dive recovery.

By the time those F6Fs were through, *Bunker Hill* and *San Jacinto* pilots picked up the scraps: a dozen Zekes, "Judys" and "Tonys" while

LCDR William A. Dean led *Hornet's* Fighting 2 during the First Battle of the Philippine Sea. (U.S. Naval Inst.)

Princeton's VF-27 not only had the fleet's most unique markings, it was the top-scoring light carrier squadron of the battle. "Sweet P's" Hellcats were credited with 30 victories on 19 June 1944. (Author's coll. via R.M. Hill)

several VF-10 "Grim Reapers" intercepted a torpedo attack on TG58.7 and broke up the effort.

But whatever the novice Japanese aviators lacked in ability, they did not lack for courage. A handful pressed on to attack Lee's battlewagons, west of the carrier groups. Lt. Don Gordon, an *Enterprise* fighter pilot, described TG58.7 as "an attractive, lethal target." He was right: one enemy pilot scored a hit on *South Dakota* (BB-57) which did no harm. To "Flash" Gordon, the view of *Indiana* (BB-58) steaming in the center of a six-mile circle of 23 other warships beneath a 20,000-foot flak umbrella was "my most memorable scene in WW II."

Task force radar put the "raid count" at 50-plus, and American claims exceeded Air Group 653's actual 42 losses. But though three F6F pilots were killed (including a VF-25 aviator), the fighter pilots and their controllers had performed superbly, gaining local superiority over the 64 raiders with 74 Hellcats.

Their abilities were about to be tested again.

THUNDER BELOW

Things had already gone wrong for Ozawa. A five-boat wolfpack west of the Marianas included USS *Albacore* (SS-218) under Cdr. J.W. Blanchard. He had been in contact with the Japanese force almost an hour when, at 0910, *Albacore* fired six torpedoes at the most lucrative target: HMIJS *Taiho*. It was an inopportune moment, as Ozawa's flagship was launching her second strike of the morning. Committed to her course into the wind, she was entirely vulnerable.

One of *Taiho's* 42 assigned pilots alertly noted the white wakes closing his ship and reacted instantly. Flight Warrant Officer Sakio Komatsu shoved his stick forward and expertly smashed his D4Y "Judy" into the torpedo's path. In the U.S. Navy he would have received a posthumous Medal of Honor. Imperial Japan, with a different standard of heroism, regarded such sacrifice as routine.

Still, one of *Albacore's* "fish" connected, jamming *Taiho's* forward elevator and wrenching some fuel and water lines. Flight operations continued without immediate concern—a confidence that would prove badly misplaced.

American submarines weren't finished with CarDivOne. During the noon hour Lt. Cdr. H.J. Kossler maneuvered *Cavalla* (SS-244) into position and put three torpedoes into *Shokaku*. Almost three hours later, while her assailant was escaping, she erupted in a fuel-fed explosion and went down by the bow. "Flying Crane" took some 1,200 men and nine planes to the bottom of the Mariana Basin.

Within several minutes *Taiho's* ticking time bomb detonated. Fuel vapors had been allowed to circulate throughout the flagship, and the effect was disastrous. However, "Giant Phoenix" was longer dying than *Shokaku* and sank with fewer men but 13 aircraft. Having previously lost seven carriers in two years, the Imperial Navy still had much to learn about damage control.

RAID II

The second strike, from CarDiv One, originally numbered 130 aircraft. However, aborts and casualties inflicted by nervous Japanese gunners reduced the effectives to 109 Zekes, Judys and Jills by the time they strobed on *Lexington's* radar at 1107. Though Cdr. Paul Buie's "Airdales" were vectored outbound, *Essex* fighters got there first.

Led by CAG David McCampbell, three divisions of "Fabled Fifteen" (minus two "air aborts" that remained overhead *Essex*) jumped on Air Group 601 some 40 miles west of the battleships. While four Hellcats tied up the Zeke top cover at 20,000 feet, McCampbell took his other six into the lower Judys, stacked in a formation some 1,200 feet deep. Flying two-plane sections, making fast high-side runs, VF-15 began depleting the raiders.

Related McCampbell, "My first target was a Judy on the left flank approximately halfway back in the formation. It was my...intention after completing this run...to pass under it, retire across the formation and take under fire a plane on the right flank with a low-side attack. These plans became upset when the first plane blew up, practically in my face, and caused a pullout above the entire formation. I remember being unable to get to the other side fast enough, feeling as though every rear gunner had his fire directed at me.

"My second attack was made on a Judy on the right flank...which burned favorably on one pass and fell away...out of control. Retirement was made below and ahead: my efforts were directed towards retaining as much speed as possible and working myself ahead and into position for an attack on the leader.

"A third pass was made from below rear on a Judy which was hit and smoking as he pulled out and down from the formation. Retirement was made by pulling up and to the side, which placed me in position for an above-rear run on the leader (who was) closely formed with his port wingman, the other wingman trailing somewhat right rear. While reaching for a favorable position on the leader, it was noted that the formation really consisted of two groups, the lower one being laterally displaced about 1,000 yards and about 500 feet below. After my first pass on the leader with no visible damage...pullout was made below and to the left. Seeing it would be easier to concentrate on the port wingman...my next pass was an above-rear run from seven o'clock, causing the wingman to explode in an envelope of flames.

"Breaking away down and to the left placed me in position for a below-rear run on the leader from five o'clock, after which I worked onto his tail and continued to fire until he burned furiously and spiralled downward out of control. During the last bursts on the leader, gun stoppages occurred. Both port and starboard guns were charged in an attempt to get them firing again.

"A brief survey of the situation at this point revealed that the formation had been decimated and the attack effectively broken up. One Judy who apparently had been leading the lower formation...offered himself as a target to me, at this time being four o'clock down. A modified high-side run was made on him. Only my starboard guns fired, which threw me into a violent skid and an early pullout was made. Guns were charged twice again, and since my target had pushed over and gained high speed, a stern chase ensued. Bursts of my starboard guns alone, before all guns ceased to fire, caused him to burn and pull into a high wingover before plummeting into the sea. Neither the pilot nor rear-seat man bailed out before the plane struck the water and disintegrated. While witnessing this crash, further efforts were made to clear the gun stoppages without success, and it was naturally assumed that all ammo had been expended. Acting on this assumption, I returned and orbited over base."

Three VF-15 ensigns claimed nine more bombers while at least four Zekes also went down. It was not all one-sided, however, as Ens. Ralph Foltz, after bagging two Judys, had to push his throttle "through the gate" for water injection to outrun a threatening Zeke. Ens. Claude Plant had an even tougher time. A skillful Japanese pilot clung to Plant's tail, putting 7.7 and 20mm rounds in the Hellcat's tough hide before another F6F shot the assailant off his tail. When Plant trapped aboard *Essex*, he counted some 150 holes in his plane, including one through each propeller blade. One VF-15 pilot, Ens. G.H. Rader, never came back at all.

Lt. Alex Vraciu of VF-16 became the Navy's top fighter ace in the Marianas. Six Judy dive-bombers on the 19th and a Zero the following day ran his tally to 19 confirmed victories. (Author's coll.)

However, by the time the combat drifted eastward, McCampbell's pilots were treated to the unforgettable sight of vari-colored parachutes dangling in midair or mingling with oil slicks and wreckage on the surface of the sea.

Forty-three more Hellcats piled in minutes later, half of them from VF-16. Climbing at full power, pulling 52 inches of mercury from their R-2800s, not all the F6Fs could keep up. One of the stragglers in Buie's propwash was Lt(jg) Alex Vraciu, whose supercharger was stuck in low blower. Additionally, his windscreen was coated with a film of oil, reducing visibility. But rather than miss the fight, Vraciu called his fighter director and requested a vector for his four-plane division.

"The FDO directed us to vector 265 degrees. There was something in his voice that indicated he had a good one on the string. The bogies were 75 miles away when reported, and we headed out, hopeful of meeting them halfway. I saw two other groups of Hellcats converging from starboard--four in one group, three in the other.

"About 25 miles away, I tallyhoed three bogeys and closed toward them. In the back of my mind I figured, 'There's got to be more than three planes,' remembering the seriousness in the FDO's voice. Spot-gazing intently, I suddenly picked out a large, rambling mass of at least 50 planes 2,000 feet below on the port side. My adrenalin flow hit high C! They were about 35 miles from our ships, heading in fast. I remember thinking that this could

develop into a once-in-a-lifetime fighter pilot's dream.

"Then, a little puzzled and suspicious, I looked about for the fighter cover that normally would be overhead, but there did not seem to be a top cover. By this time we were in perfect position for a high-side run. Giving a slight rock of the wings, I began a run on the nearest straggler, a Judy dive-bomber.

"However, peripherally, I was conscious of another Hellcat seeming to have designs on that Jap also; he was too close for comfort, almost blindsided, so I aborted my run. There were enough cookies on this plate for everyone. I streaked underneath the formation, getting a good look at the planes for the first time. They were Judys, Jills and Zeros. I radioed an amplified report.

"After pulling up and over, I picked out another Judy on the edge of the formation. It was doing some mild maneuvering and the rear gunner was squirting away as I came down from astern. I worked in close and gave him a burst. He caught fire quickly and headed down to the sea, trailing a long plume of smoke.

"I pulled up again and found two more Judys flying a loose wing. I came in from the rear, sending one down burning. Dipping the Hellcat's wing, I slid over on the one slightly ahead and got it on the same pass. It caught fire also, and I could see the gunner still peppering away at me as he disappeared in an increasing sharp arc downward.

"That made three down, and we were now getting close to the fleet. The enemy planes had been pretty well chopped down, but a substantial number remained. It didn't look like we would score a grand slam. I reported this info back to base.

"The sky appeared full of smoke and pieces of planes, and we were trying to ride herd on the remainder to keep them from scattering.

"Another meatball broke formation up ahead, and I slid onto his tail, again working in close because of my oil-smeared windshield. I gave him a short burst but it was enough; it went right into the sweet spot at the root of his wing tanks. The pilot or control cables must have been hit, also, because the burning plane twisted crazily out of control.

"In spite of our efforts, the Jills were beginning to descend for their torpedo runs and the remaining Judys were at the point of peeling off to go down with their bombs. I headed for a group of three Judys in a long column. By the time I reached the tail-ender, we were almost over the outer destroyer screen but still fairly high. The first

Judy was about to begin his dive, and as he started to nose over, I noticed a black puff beside him. Our five-inchers were beginning to open up.

"Foolishly, maybe, I overtook the nearest one. It seemed that I scarcely touched the trigger and his engine started coming to pieces. The Judy started smoking, then torching alternately off and on, as it disappeared below.

"The next one was about one-fifth of the way down in his dive--apparently trying for one of our destroyers--before I caught up with him. This time a short burst produced astonishing results. He blew up with a tremendous explosion right in front of my face. I had seen planes blow up before, but never like this.

"I yanked up sharply to avoid the scattered pieces and flying hot stuff, then radioed, 'Splash number six! There's one more ahead and he's diving on a BB. But I don't think he'll make it.'

"Hardly had the words left my mouth than the Judy caught a direct hit. He had run into a solid curtain of steel from the battlewagon.

A Nakajima B5N Kate, set afire by anti-aircraft batteries of TF 58, heads for a watery crash landing on June 19, 1944. (National Archives via U.S. Naval Inst.)

A VF-31 Hellcat misses *Cabot*'s arresting wires en route to a barrier engagement. (Author's coll.)

"Looking around, only six Hellcats seemed to be in the sky. Glancing backward from where we had come, in a pattern 35 miles long, there were only flaming oil slicks on the water."

Vraciu had consumed merely eight minutes and 360 machine-gun rounds to splash six Judys and break up the attack. His squadronmates returned to Lex, reporting 15 more. When he landed back aboard to a tumultuous welcome, Vraciu also learned that he had flown the mission with his F6F's wing locks partly exposed!

A damaged B6N Kate on its way down. (National Archives)

As before, the Japanese split their force, dissipating the effect of their attack. Besides Lee's battleships--still nearest the enemy--two carrier groups also were assailed. However, *Yorktown* dealt with this phase of the attack as CAG J.M. Peters and VF-1 skipper B.M. Strean waded in with 21 fighters. Their five divisions were dispersed vertically through 25,000 feet of altitude, following radar vectors as high as 30,000 in pursuit of Zekes. The Yorktowners returned to "Coal Base" exuberant, claiming 32 kills among 35 bandits for one pilot and plane, plus two other F6Fs written off.

Persistent Japanese got through, however, making individual or small-scale attacks on four battlewagons and four flattops. Only one ship was directly hit, as *Indiana* shrugged off a Jill that destroyed itself against her armored hull. In TG58.2 six Judys near-missed *Bunker Hill*, inflicting 73 wounded, and dropped a phosphorous bomb overhead *Wasp* that killed one sailor. An ineffectual torpedo attack against 58.3 targeted *Enterprise* and *Princeton* but accomplished nothing, thanks to those ships' fighters. The "Grim Reapers" got a vector on the inbound Jills but VF-27's new executive officer got there first. Lt. W.B. Lamb already had bagged two Jills when he latched onto a formation of 12 more. Pacing the speedy "torpeckers," he radioed their position and called for help before attacking--with one gun working. He claimed two more and a probable before VF-10 dispersed the rest.

The 20 Japanese pilots who returned to CarDiv One reported damage to several American ships but in truth they inflicted small loss: VF-1's casualties plus one pilot and plane each from VF-14 and -15 and a Fighting Eight aircraft. TF58 had concentrated 162 Hellcats against 109 raiders, probably destroying 80-plus versus claims of 100 or more.

RAID III

The third raid was almost a non-event. CarDiv Two had launched a 49-plane strike shortly past 1000; it wandered around a goodly part of the Pacific, bedeviled by inept navigation by the scouts and poor communications. Only the fighter escorts found the target, and the 16 Zekes were immediately pummeled by 17 Hellcats of VF-1 and -2. At 1304 a short, sharp dogfight began 60 miles northwest of the task force, with six of the *Hornet* pilots claiming nine kills and a probable. The "Red Rippers" actually splashed seven, with one F6F damaged.

RAID IV

At 1100 CarDiv One and Two sent up 82 planes which, like Raid I, suffered from poor scouting. Sent to a point 100 miles southwest of Guam, they found nothing and split apart. The *Zuikaku* contribution (18 planes) returned to base while CarDiv Two's contingent made for Rota and Guam. Sixteen Judys and Zekes of Air Group 652 passed within sight of Montgomery's unit and attempted an attack on *Wasp* and *Bunker Hill*. AA gunners splashed five.

Lt. Zenji Abe, a veteran of Pearl Harbor and Dutch Harbor, led the dive bombers of 652 Kokutai from Carrier Division Two. He managed to land on Rota Island. He is shown here in 1941 by his Aichi D3A Val. (J.W. Lambert coll. via Zenji Abe)

The venerable Douglas Dauntless was a key U.S. Navy weapon in WW II. The designation SBD was said by its crews to stand for "slow but deadly". This Dash 5, Bureau No. 35982, was the aircraft of LCDR Jim Ramage, CO of VB-10, flying from *Enterprise*.

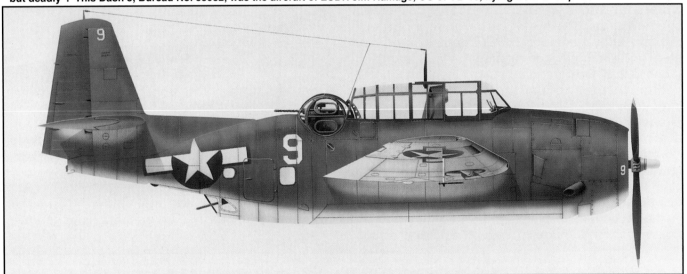

This TBF-1C Grumman Avenger, Bureau No. 24241, was assigned to Lt. (jg) Warren R. Omark, VT-24, of aircraft carrier *Belleau Wood,* and took part in the sinking of HIMJS *Hiyo* on 20 June 1944.

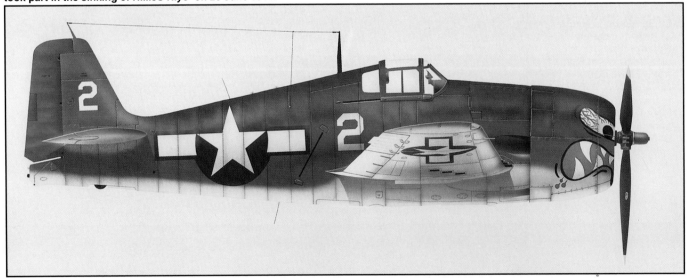

This Grumman Hellcat, Bureau No. 40832, was a very late model F6F-3, already bearing some of the changes that would be standard in the Dash 5. It served with VF-27 aboard *Princeton*. Fighting 27 was the only Navy squadron known to employ the "sharks mouth" motif, common to the RAF, AVG and many USAAF units.

The famous Mitsubishi Zero was also built at Nakajima, as was this A6M5c which flew from the carrier *Taiho* as part of 601 Kokutai, 311 Hikotai.

The long serving Aichi Val dive bomber was obsolete but still in use in June 1944 and throughout the Pacific war. The D3A2 displayed here was part of Air Group 652, Hikotai 321 off the *Junyo*.

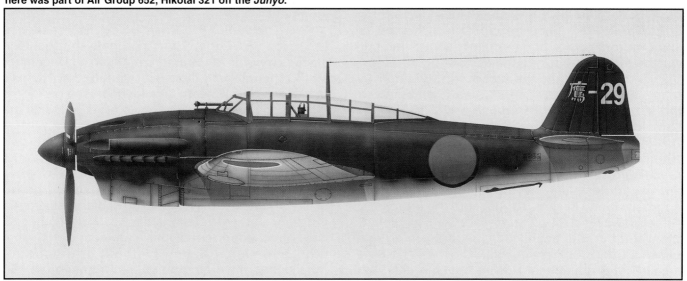

This sleek, in-line, carrier type Yokosuka D4Y1 Judy dive bomber and recon aircraft was part of the Marianas' shore based air contingent, stationed on Tinian Island. A late production model actually built by Aichi, this particular aircraft bears the markings of the 523 Kokutai. The Kanji symbol on the tail means "Taka" or Hawk.

The rest of CarDiv Two's formation made for Orote Field, presumably a safe haven on Guam. It was like a hen seeking cover in a fox's lair. Forty-one Hellcats from *Essex, Hornet, Enterprise* and *Cowpens* dropped into Orote's traffic pattern shortly past 1600 and shot down at least 30. The Hellcat pilots claimed twice that number, but another 19 were considered damaged beyond repair.

In 1993 one of Air Group 652's senior aviators related his impression of the massacre. Lt. Zenji Abe, a dive-bomber veteran of Pearl Harbor and beyond, was awed by the swarms of F6Fs that chewed his formation to pieces. Still wide-eyed at the memory, he exclaimed, "I never see so many Grummans!"

Some Hellcat pilots also were awed at the opportunity. Lt. Russell R. Reiserer, an old hand around the Pacific, had flown with VF-10 in 1942-43. Now, leading a flight of dual-shift night-fighter pilots from *Hornet*, he latched onto a string of Vals and lowered his landing gear and flaps in order to execute five.

Reiserer's shipmate, Ens. W.B. Webb, was a former enlisted pilot just five days past his 24th birthday. Though "Spider" Webb had never scored before, he made the most of his opportunity. He radioed, "I have 40 Jap planes surrounded and need a little help!" Before reinforcements arrived he joined the enemy traffic pattern and, despite malfunctioning guns, in a matter of minutes claimed six Vals destroyed and two probables.

Others also were racking up multiple kills. *Essex* CAG Dave McCampbell, back after his big sortie against Raid II, tangled with three Zekes. He quickly bagged one but the second proved capable and smart. Alone and down low, unable to out-turn the A6M, McCampbell dropped his belly tank and bent the throttle toward Orote Point, hollering for help. Three F6Fs shot the pursuer off his tail--a favor he returned to another pilot minutes later. It was his seventh victory of the day. His fighter exec, Lt. Cdr. J.F. Rigg, and the rest of VF-15 added 11 more. FitRons 10, 28 and 51 also contributed to the carnage, though *Enterprise* and *San Jacinto* each lost a pilot.

The VF-10 loss was Lt. H.C. Clem, the "Reapers'" exec, killed trying to protect an SOC rescuing a downed flier. He engaged two Zeros strafing the floatplane, but the Japanese leader was aggressive and skilled. Turning into the attack, Lt. Shimazu Ozaki of 343 *Kokutai* shot Clem's F6F into the water but was bounced by another *Enterprise* pilot. Lt. Cdr. R.E. Harmer was CO of VF(N)-101, a small F4U-2 detachment doing daytime duty like his F6F-3N counterparts. Harmer, who had first fought from *Saratoga* in 1942, got a brief shot at Ozaki, whose plane made off streaming smoke.

Forty years later, researchers established that the Japanese ace died of wounds after landing on Guam. The SOC took off safely and returned to the task force.

Essex drew part of the island CAP until dusk, and McCampbell cornered Cdr. Brewer, the VF-15 skipper. Relating his own experience, CAG-15 told Brewer to take his formation in high "and be extra cautious."

On station at 1825, Brewer spotted some planes trying to land on Guam. He led his wingman down to attack and bagged one for his fifth kill of the day. But in doing so he lost his altitude safety net. High-flying Zekes dropped down on the *Essex* section, killing Brewer and Ens. Thomas Tarr. The other VF-15 pilots claimed eight more kills, but considered it a poor exchange.

The last combat came 35 minutes later as a *San Jacinto* division made an intercept 30 miles from the task group. Lt(jg) S.H. Bobb of VF-51 got a shot at a single-engine bogey and claimed a probable. America's greatest air battle was over.

RADIO AND RADAR

The events of 19 June proved conclusively--if proof were still needed--the importance of electronics in modern naval warfare. Almost every ship in TF58 had its own combat information center (CIC) with specially-trained fighter direction officers (FDOs) managing a team of radar operators. The air-defense network was layered vertically, from individual ships to their respective task group commanders to the task force fighter director in Mitscher's flagship. In order to work properly, the system demanded technical expertise, reliable equipment--and fast, accurate judgment.

The senior FDO was a New York reservist, Lt. Joseph R. Eggert, who had held that position since *Lexington* left Bremerton, Wash. in December 1943. Though not officially assigned to Mitscher's staff, Eggert's CIC team functioned as the task force director, handing off contacts to other ships as the need arose.

By mid-1943 the Pacific Fleet had two air-search radars, the older SC-2 and the somewhat newer SK set. A few carriers, including *Lexington*, mounted new SM height-finders which better discriminated not only the altitudes of target aircraft, but their vertical relationships to one another as well. Atmospheric conditions were near-perfect that day, as "skin paints" (without transponder amplification) were made on aircraft as far as 150 miles away, at almost any altitude.

However, radar information was of little use if it could not reliably be passed to the ultimate "consumers" of that data: airborne fighter pilots. Relatively new four-channel VHF radios were standard equipment in F6F-3s, permitting simultaneous communication between ships (usually CICs), between FDOs and CAPs, or between CICs, air plots and other aircraft, such as antisubmarine patrols. At the time of Operation FORAGER, TF58 was still converting to the new gear, with only two of the planned four channels common to all ships and air groups. Though some frequencies became extremely crowded during the day, radio discipline held.

Vice Adm. Mitscher was lavish in his praise of the CIC teams which conducted a near-perfect defense of the task force. In part he wrote:

"The four major attacks were each hit at ranges of some 50-60 miles from the carriers, and each time with sufficient altitude advantage to our fighters. It was the first time that a major enemy air blow has been made on our forces without the loss of or serious damage to at least one of our carriers. It proved that the long and costly efforts in research, training, and the practical application of radar have not been in vain."

Furthermore, CTF58 emphasized two factors that contributed to so successful an air-defense doctrine:

"(First) every effort was made to insure that an adequate number of fighters were being vectored against each raid...

"(Secondly) insofar as possible, every effort was made to insure that an adequate supply of fresh fighters was available for any subsequent raids...

"Of 33 interceptions initiated as a result of radar or visual contact, 28 were completed successfully...One of the most important factors in the success of fighter direction during this phase was the instantaneous reinforcement of standing combat air patrols. Whenever one division of the standing two-division combat air patrol was committed to an interception, eight more fighters were immediately launched if another bogey contact appeared on the radars."

While the Japanese made some effort at electronic countermeasures--dropping aluminum strips intended to cloud American radar scopes--the effect was minimal. Efficient use of "window" required knowledge of enemy radar frequencies, and Ozawa's aviators apparently lacked sufficient knowledge of TF58 electronics as well as quantity of chaff. At any rate, the ECM effort was ineffective.

RECKONING

Though intermittent, the air battle had lasted some 13 hours, start to finish. Ships' crews were almost constantly at battle stations--*Monterey*, for instance, went to general quarters seven times during the day. In that period, 206 Hellcat pilots were credited with 371 confirmed victories. Six became "aces in a day," including two who had never scored before. Thirteen were killed during intercepts and searches while another fell victim to nervous American anti-aircraft gunners.

But the battle was not limited to repelling Ozawa's four raids, and neither were the losses. TF58 lost six bombers and two fighters to flak over

Enterprise's night fighter detachment of VF(N)-101 engaged enemy scouts during FORAGER preliminaries on 15 June, then were thrown into the daylight battle on 19 June. Standing (l. to r.) Ens. Poirer, Ens. Brunson, Det. CO LCDR Dick Harmer, radar fighter director, Lt. Orphanides, Ens. Roulen. Kneeling (l. to r.) Lt.(jg) R.F. Holden, Ens. Kelly, Ens. Von Sprecken. (R.E.Harmer)

28

Leading *Essex's* Air Group 15, CDR Davic McCampbell shot down seven Japanese aircraft in two sorties on 19 June. Fighting 15 ended the day with sixty-eight and one-half shootdowns, a record at the time. McCampbell's final tally was thirty-four confirmed victories. (Author's coll.)

Guam, while six more planes were destroyed operationally. In all, Mitscher lost 27 pilots or aircrewmen from 18 fighters and 12 bombers. Additionally, 31 officers and sailors had been killed aboard task force ships.

Excluding 19 aborts, Ozawa's carriers had launched 328 planes against TF58; perhaps 25 broke through the CAPs. The optimistic young Japanese often reported as much what they wished to see as what they actually observed, and Ozawa believed them. His report stated, "it is certain" that four or five carriers and a battleship or large cruiser were sunk or damaged, while 160 American planes were thought shot down.

In fairness to Ozawa and his command, the immense margin of error was not unusual in the Imperial Navy. Two years previously, Vice Adm. Nagumo's Zero pilots had reported meeting dozens of American fighters in the Midway attack, claiming 40 "confirmed" destroyed and many more "probables." In fact, only 25 had scrambled from Midway, of which 15 were lost.

While the Hellcat pilots overclaimed, their margin of error was vastly less than their opponents. The F6Fs, with some help from search planes and the CVEs, had deprived Ozawa of some 300 carrier aircraft and floatplanes (destroyed or rendered unflyable), plus several more Guam-based planes. TF58 gunners accounted for upwards of 20 more. Additionally, 22 planes sank with *Shokaku* and *Taiho*.

According to Morison, Ozawa had begun the battle with 43 floatplanes; at dawn the next day he had 27 operational and presumably six inoperable--a net loss of ten. This tracks extremely well with TF58's claims of nine confirmed. However, the far-flung "battle of the scouts" lent itself to accurate reporting because of the very small numbers involved.

At day's end, debriefings were still in progress aboard every carrier. At some point aboard *Lexington*, Lt(jg) "Ziggy" Neff described the events as "an old-time turkey shoot." Neff had been credited with four kills in two missions that day--the only time he scored during the war. But his phrase, apparently related by Cdr. Buie to Adm. Mitscher, made its way into history.

A Grumman FM-2 Wildcat of VC-10, badly damaged in landing aboard *Gambier Bay* is about to be pushed over the side. Wildcats from two escort carriers contributed to the aerial victories of 19 June 1944. (National Archives via Tailhook Association)

20 JUNE 1944 – THE PURSUIT

The Turkey Shoot may have been the highlight of the battle, but it was definitely not the end. On Tuesday the 20th, Mitscher's search teams finally found Ozawa withdrawing westward. It had been a frustrating situation: both submarines and patrol planes had located the Mobile Fleet the day before, but TF58 was hampered by delay in receipt of the messages and some confusion as to priority. Had Spruance known Ozawa's exact location on the 19th, there would have been two complications: Mitscher could not launch a worthwhile strike without seriously depleting his Force CAP, and to do so would leave the landings vulnerable to counterattack. Years later, Spruance patiently explained to a former squadron commander that admirals also take orders; guarding the amphibian vessels was his primary mission.

Whatever the problems, at 1538 two *Enterprise* TBFs made visual contact and began tracking the Mobile Fleet.

"LAUNCH 'EM"

Three task groups began launching 240 aircraft at 1624. However, aborts reduced the total to 227 effectives: 96 fighters, 54 Avengers and 77 dive-bombers, including 26 SBDs off *Enterprise* and *Lexington*. While elements of eleven air groups climbed outbound, a second deck-load strike was being prepared on most of the engaged carriers as well as the "stay-at-homes": *Essex, Langley, Cowpens* and *Princeton*. However, as darkness approached the second launch was scrubbed.

The strike package was heavily weighted toward the CVs: *Yorktown,* for instance, contributed 36 planes while CVL *San Jacinto* launched two TBMs. Flagship *Lexington's* contribution was representative of TF58 aviators, as Lex's 30 pilots and 27 aircrewmen averaged 24 years of age, with extremes of 19 to 43. They hailed from 25 of the 48 states: nine from California, six from Massachusetts, five from New York, four from Ohio. Some were superstitious to the point of carrying multiple talismans. One SBD gunner would not fly without his lucky charms: a pipe, an ivory die, one screwdriver, two nuts and bolts--plus a pine-cone "worry bird."

LT. Robert Nelson (above, center) with crew members (l. to r.) Gruebel and Livingston and Lt. (jg) James Moore (below, center) with crew members (l. to r.) Watts and Hovis, all of VT-10 were the first to locate and shadow the Japanese Mobile Fleet. (Bill Balden)

Members of VT-28 review the attack plan with skipper Gift prior to launch from *Monterey* on June 20, 1944. Front row, kneeling (l. to r.): AMM 1/c John C. Cason, Lt. Ronald P. Gift and Ens. Robert W. Burnett. Back row, standing, (l. to r.): Ens. Thomas G. Dreis, ARM 3/c J.P. Mitchell, AOM 2/c Kenneth H. Mast, ARM 2/c Richard P. Goerlitz, ARM 3/c William E. Trego, ARM 2/c D.A. Raulston, AOM 3/c D.F. Riley, AOM 2/c Allen J. Rogers, Lt. (jg) Paul G. Pennoyer. (Mrs. Abbie M. Rogers)

Though the target was enemy warships, bombs were the weapon of choice--even F6Fs lugged single 500-pounders. The ordnance selection reflected previous experience, as American aerial torpedoes had proven maddening over the first two years of war. The U.S. Navy's torpedo scandal of WW II was the result of prewar complacency, bureaucratic inertia and absurd budget constraints--no empirical tests were conducted until months after Pearl Harbor. But this evening, though only about 20 Avengers carried torpedoes, they would prove their worth.

Aside from tactical considerations--even more than Japanese opposition--everyone's concern was fuel. The mission was briefed as a long-range strike of 240 nautical miles, prompting serious discussion in every ready room. Cruise control was paramount--a slow climb to altitude with careful attention to fuel mixture and power settings for the duration of the fight.

However, another complication arose. One of the VT-10 search pilots found a one-degree error in the original report: almost another 60 miles of longitude. The airborne attack groups got the word

after launch: they would fly more than 300 nautical miles into the westering sun, and nearly that far back to the task force.

Leading VB-10 in the *Enterprise* formation, Lt. Cdr. J.D. Ramage nursed his "Slow But Deadly" SBDs at 140 knots:

"Strike groups were passing us until we were all alone in the rear of some 220 aircraft. We had our own game plan. I began to even out the fuel in my wings by shifting tanks about every 15 minutes. I did not want to have an asymmetrical load in my dive. Also, we had been warned that one wanted at least some fuel in each tank. A completely empty tank was considered more likely to explode because of residual vapor.

"About an hour and 45 minutes out (260 nm) I sighted a strike group off to port in an attack situation. Beneath them I could see four oilers and several escorts. I broke radio silence, calling to Lt. Van Eason, our torpedo leader. 'Eighty-Five Sniper from 41 Sniper. We will not attack. The Charlie Victors (CVs) are dead ahead.' Then I opened up on VHF guard channel, saying, 'Unknown strike leader from 41 Sniper. The Charlie Victors are dead

Besides VB-10 aboard *Enterprise*, Bombing 16 on Admiral Mitscher's flagship, *Lexington*, was the only other dive-bomber squadron in TF 58 still flying Douglas SBDs by June 1944. The Curtiss SB2C Helldiver began replacing the Dauntless late in 1943. (Author's coll. via R. M. Hill)

ahead. What are you trying to do? Sink their merchant marine?' The unknown strike group continued with its attack despite our instructions that the Japanese carriers were the prime targets. I was exasperated. Later I found that the SB2Cs were low on fuel, but who wasn't?

"Radio discipline was not good. I could hear all sorts of completely unwarranted transmissions from over the target area. Well, at least the Japanese carriers were located."

A Grumman F6F-3 Hellcat of VF-1 prepares to launch from *Yorktown*. Message on blackboard gives late target bearing and distance. (National Archives via U.S. Naval Inst.)

Aircraft carrier *Zuikaku* and escorts under a rain of bombs from VB-2 on June 20, 1944 west of the Marianas Islands.   Damaged and afire, the Japanese carrier survived the battle but lived for only four more months.   (National Archives)

ATTACK ON THE MOBILE FLEET

The first Japanese sighting of TF58 planes came at 1825. Within minutes the Mobile Fleet had some 68 interceptors airborne--by itself a substantial number but too few to defend four separate task groups spread across miles of ocean.

Mitscher's aviators found the Mobile Fleet dispersed by carrier divisions. They were arrayed roughly northeast-southwest, partially hidden by two huge cumulus clouds that glowed yellow-red in the lowering light. Aside from the formation that attacked the Japanese oilers, the other air groups went after "the fighting navy." In all, elements of seven air groups exchanged gunfire with the Japanese CAP, and 20 American aircraft were lost to fighters and flak--one-third of the Japanese claims. The Helldivers proved particularly vulnerable, as eight of the 51 launched were shot down. The defenders also downed seven Hellcats, four Avengers and a Dauntless--including write-offs from battle damage.

Belleau Wood had launched eight F6Fs and four TBFs of Air Group 24, which concentrated on CarDiv Two. During the approach, Ens. W.D. Luton delivered his attack on *Junyo* or *Ryuho* as Lt. George Brown led the other two toward *Hiyo*. One of Brown's wingmen, Lt. (jg) Warren Omark described the attack on the 24,000-ton *Hiyo*.

Lt. George Brown with crewmen Platz (left) and Babcock. Brown led VT-24 to the *Hiyo* where his Avenger was badly damaged by Japanese AA. With the plane apparently afire and communications with Brown severed, Platz and Babcock parachuted. After the attack the plane was seen flying for a time by others from Torpedo 24. (B.C. Tate)

The four crews of VT-24 which participated in the sinking of Japanese aircraft carrier *Hiyo* late on 20 June 1944. Back row, left to right: Pilots Lt. (jg) W.R. Omark, Lt. (jg) B.C. Tate, Ens. W.D. Luton, and (inset) Lt. (jg) G.P. Brown who was lost on the mission. Crewmen, left to right: John E. Prince, Robert E. Ranes, James Dobbs, George Platz, Philip Whiting, James Brookbank, and Ellis Babcock. Not pictured, John F. Siwicki. (B.C. Tate)

Six Grumman Avengers of VT-2 penetrate cumulus clouds near TF 58. *Hornet* provided a half-dozen TBMs to the afternoon strike on 20 June. (R.M. Hill)

"Brownie, Ben Tate and I fanned out to approach from different angles. The attack course took us over the outlying screen of destroyers, then cruisers and finally the battleships. This screen had to be penetrated in order to reach the proper range for launching torpedoes against the carrier. The anti-aircraft fire was very intense and I took as much evasive action as I could.

"During the attack, Brownie's aircraft was hit by AA and caught fire. I think one of the remarkable stories of the war then took place. AMM 2/c G.H. Platz and ARM 2/c E.C. Babcock were Brownie's crewmen and, knowing their plane was afire and unable to reach Brownie on the intercom, they parachuted and actually witnessed the attack from the water. They remained there all night and were found and rescued the next day by search planes from our task force.

"We came in at about 400 feet from the water to get a satisfactory launch of our torpedoes and dropped them on converging courses which presumably did not allow the enemy carrier to take effective evasive action. Platz and Babcock later reported that we did hit the carrier and that it later sank."

Obviously upset at the successful attack on *Hiyo*, Zekes chased the Avengers in futile anger. However, Tate and Omark evaded the CAP and independently came across Lt. Brown's blackened, battle-damaged Avenger. Brown was flying slowly, just above the water. "He held up his right arm," recalled Tate, "which was all bloodstained. I tried to keep him on my wing to guide him back. I called him on the radio but he didn't answer with anything understandable. I lost him in the dark."

Omark was the last to see Brown: "Brownie acted stunned, like a football player who had been hit in the head. I turned on my lights to help him, but evidently his light system was shot because he didn't turn on his. I lost him in the dark about an hour later."

Brown was never seen again. Tate and Luton both successfully ditched their battle damaged Avengers near TF58 ships. Only Omark managed to land aboard his carrier with just two gallons of gas remaining.

Hornet's Bombing Two launched 14 Curtiss Helldivers on the strike of 20 June, more than any other SB2C squadron. (R.M. Hill)

Among the pilots attacking CarDivOne–northernmost of Ozawa's units–was Lt. H.E. Buell of Bombing Two. Hal Buell knew his way around the Pacific, having flown SBDs from three carriers during 1942. A veteran of Coral Sea and nearly all the Guadalcanal naval-air battles, he now led one wing of *Hornet's* Helldivers down on *Zuikaku*:

"As I pushed over into my dive at about 12,000 feet, the AA fire became so intense...that I saw no way of getting through it. My dive brakes were already open and I was well into a good dive, but because of the potent defensive fire, I felt like I was moving in slow motion in quicksand...At this point I did something I had never done before in a dive--I closed my dive brakes. My plane responded by dropping like a stone toward the target below, leaving the heavy AA fire behind.

"My speed was building up and, in the clean condition without flaps, I could never expect to pull...out of the dive...Shouting a prayer to my guardian angel, at 6,000 feet I placed the dive brake selector back into the open position. The wing brakes did what no manufacturing specs said they would--they opened! It was as if a giant hand grabbed my plane by the tail; my headlong plunge slowed, and there was the enemy carrier dead in my sight below me, turning into my flight path along its lengthwise axis. At a point-blank range of 2,000 feet, I fired my bomb."

Buell's choice of words is illuminating. He regarded a dive-bomber as a precision weapon much like a sniper's rifle, but in the dusk and confusion he could not "call his shot." However, Buell's Helldiver took a hit--a heavy-caliber round that set the starboard wing afire and sent a splinter into the pilot's back.

Reducing airspeed, Buell got the fire extinguished and navigated back to the task force. There, fighting for low-speed control of his stricken airplane, he made a crash landing aboard *Lexington*. After medical attention and a debriefing withMitscher's staff, Buell wound up rooming with a VF-16 pilot--Lt. Jim Seybert, a former high school friend from Ottumwa, Iowa.

Of Ozawa's seven surviving carriers on the 20th, *Hiyo* succumbed to torpedo damage, taking Capt. Yokoi and much of her crew with her. The others got off lightly: *Junyo* (two bomb hits), *Zuikaku* (one) and *Chiyoda* (one) while *Ryuho* had slight damage from near misses. Additionally, two oilers were sunk while battleship *Haruna* took a bomb and cruiser *Maya* sustained several close misses.

TF58 aircrews reported 67 Japanese planes destroyed or damaged over the Mobile Fleet, one-third of those by Air Group 16. One Zeke

Lt. Hal Buell and Lt. (jg) T. Jack Taylor, both of VB-2, congratulate one another aboard *Hornet* following their dive-bombing attack on the Japanese aircraft carrier, *Zuikaku*. (Buell)

brought Alex Vraciu's tally to 19, a figure that would remain tops in the Navy for another three months. In all, the Americans claimed 27 shootdowns though Morison computed the number at 40, while the Japanese figure of 65 lost undoubtedly was a lump sum including operational attrition. Obviously, few of the survivors got back aboard in the dark.

For Mitscher's aircrews, the long return to TF-58 went into history as the "mission beyond darkness" as dozens of aircraft succumbed to fuel starvation or the confusion over the task force. Mitscher justly was lauded for his courageous decision to turn on the lights--apparently at the suggestion of his chief of staff, Capt. Arleigh Burke. Boldly ignoring the submarine threat, TF58 lit up almost every ship, reminding one SB2C pilot of "Coney Island on the Fourth of July." But therein lay an unexpected problem. Many aviators were unable to distinguish cruisers and destroyers from carriers, and the confusion was compounded.

SEVENTY PLANES DOWN

After the short, intense combat over the Mobile Fleet, 209 American aircraft headed east into the growing dark, more than 270 miles from base. However, fuel shortage and deck crashes far exceeded the efforts of the Japanese, as some 70 carrier planes went in the water that night. Of all the air groups flying the mission, probably none was shorter on fuel than *Wasp's*. The VF-14 action report distilled the factors into a terse account of that mission:

"Four divisions of fighters acted as escorts for the bombers and torpedo planes. En route to the target, Cdr. J.D. Blitch, who was leading the flight, took the group 45 miles southward to investigate a radar contact picked up by his rearseat man, which proved negative, and unfortunately consumed a lot of precious gasoline. Returning to base course, a group of fleet oilers and DDs was sighted and taken under attack...

"Now began the most dramatic part of the entire action as our planes commenced their long homeward trip, for by this time it was already beginning to get dark. Fighters, bombers and torpedo planes joined up as best they could...To those who remained aboard, that night will forever remain unforgettable as the planes came straggling back one by one to land aboard whichever carrier they could pick out in the darkness. Many of the bombers were forced to make water landings as they ran out of gas, some of them within sight of the fleet, which by this time had turned on every light to guide the pilots home. A number of planes crashed and burned within sight of the ships, and of course there were many barrier crashes and accidents aboard the carriers.

"Five of our fighter pilots made it safely back to the *Wasp*, four landed on the *Bunker Hill*, two each on the *Cabot* and *San Jacinto* and one each on the *Enterprise* and *Monterey*. One of our pilots landed safely aboard the *San Jacinto* without the compass or generator operating in his plane, and with no signal officer, barrier or landing lights on the ship--and only three gallons of gas left!"

Dozens of other pilots were not so fortunate. However, they had the unseen eye of radar watching over them, as recalled by Lt(jg) Morland in *Lexington*:

"I particularly remember the two hours of night landings. Those of us in CIC...were finding and trying to guide the planes in while keeping track of the approaching planes. I was on the dead reckoning tracer. We plotted the approach of a plane through its IFF until it disappeared from the scope. Then we circled the spot, noted the latitude and longitude, and sent the information to the flag staff. Fortunately, they did not need it. The destroyers in the screen had the info on their radars and initiated rescue procedures...(with) the floatplanes and PBMs that came in after daylight they did a remarkable job in rescuing the pilots. They deserve all the credit in the world."

Among the officers sharing that assessment was 30-year-old Lt. Cdr. Gerald Ford, assistant navigator in *Monterey*. He recalls the tension in the ship following launch of four TBMs at 1613:

"The wait was long, as it was 2030 that night before the formation turned into the wind to recover the returning planes. No one in Task Force 58 will ever forget the spectacle of these night landings that were seldom undertaken. All blackout measures were suspended. The task force ships were lighted almost as if they were peacetime ocean liners. The carriers had flight deck, landing signal, and glow lights burning. A destroyer in each task group had her 24-inch search light pointed up into the clouds to serve as a beacon, while others fired star shells periodically for the same purpose. From time to time a horrid illumination was afforded by the yellow flames of planes crashing into the water and catching fire.

"Aircraft landings on a carrier are always exciting, but that night to stand on the bridge, watching pilots bring their planes to the deck in the worst of conditions, was an unforgettable experience.

"Three of *Monterey's* planes were gotten safely aboard, plus one plane from *Lexington* and three from *Wasp*. The plane piloted by Ens. R.W. Burnett was seen in the landing circle, but failed to come in. It was assumed at the time that some other carrier must have taken it aboard."

Ens. Burnett's missing VT-28 crew included radioman ARM3/c W.E. Trego and gunner AOM2/c A.J. Rogers. With three other *Monterey* Avengers they attacked *Chiyoda* and sustained flak damage but made it back to TG58.2. However, after failed attempts to find a clear deck, their Avenger's Wright R-2600 quit cold--out of fuel. Allen Rogers recalls what happened next:

"Up to engine shutdown we had been flying just above stalling, so Pappy got her nose down to pick up some airspeed. He shortly hauled back on the stick in an attempt to pancake her in, but we had not enough altitude to regain speed. The plane fell off on her starboard wing and hit the water in that attitude.

"The landing wasn't particularly hard, and we had only minor problems exiting. Previously, I had returned to my turret so I jettisoned the escape hatch, flipped the buckle of my seatbelt and attempted to crawl out through the hatch opening. However...we were flying a 'borrowed' aircraft, and the assigned crew had neglected to adjust the belts...so I sat back down and methodically pulled on the belt until the overlap was completely out through the buckle. Then I exited onto the port wing.

"At the time it seemed as if my difficulty in getting free of that damn belt had taken an eternity. But I'm sure it didn't take more than five or six seconds at most. Even so, knowing that a ditched TBM usually floats for only 45 to 60 seconds, I was sort of in a hurry.

"By this time Pappy had left the cockpit and was on the starboard wing. We removed the life raft stowage plates, he pulling while I pushed the three-man raft out on the starboard wing. I then scrambled over the canopy and looked around for Trego. He had jettisoned the main tunnel hatch and was peering out at Pappy and me.

"Pappy was attempting to inflate the raft and, after a moment, I told him the aircraft was settling by the nose and I thought we should get clear. He agreed and tossed the rolled-up raft into the water and jumped after it. I followed him and Trego joined us. As we swam clear the plane's tail rose high in the air, paused for a moment and slipped beneath the waves.

"The destroyer *Owen* (DD-536), which we learned had been the object of our last two landing approaches, had hove to about 100 yards away with a searchlight on us the whole time. We had a little difficulty inflating the raft... climbed aboard and paddled over to the destroyer.

"Once aboard, we were permitted to take a freshwater shower. Meanwhile, our clothes were washed, dried and waiting for us when we dried ourselves down. Our .38-cal. revolvers were sent to the armory to be thoroughly cleaned of all saltwater and relubricated. We gave the weapons to members of the crew for souvenirs, declaring them 'lost' in the ditching so we would be issued new ones. A small price to pay for all the crew did for us."

LCDR James D. Ramage, Skipper of Bombing 10, emerges from the cockpit of his Douglass Dauntless. Ramage led the *Enterprise* air group in the 20 June dusk attack on the Japanese fleet. Standing far right is ARM 1/c David J. Cawley, Ramage's gunner. (J.D. Ramage)

Lt. Ronald P. Gift relaxes in the ready room back aboard *Monterey* after the hectic dusk strike against Japanese carrier forces on 20 June. Gift, leading VT-28, was part of 54 Grumman Avengers flying the mission. The main objective is still written on the blackboard. (Grumman)

Only about 150 of the planes that reached the Mobile Fleet snagged an arresting wire that night, and relatively few of them "trapped" on their home flight deck. A case in point was Lt. Cdr. Ramage of VB-10, who navigated back to the task force with the help of his radioman-gunner, ARM 1/c David Cawley, who prepared for the worst:

"I concentrated on our radar, which had a maximum range of 75 miles. Our ship could send a homing signal that we could receive on the radar. At 90 miles this signal began to show clearly in the pitch dark. We adjusted course only a few degrees and continued on. It was about 2030 and lots of the planes were going in the water, out of gas and some landing together in sections and divisions. The radio was chaos.

"We went over our ditching checklist. We both agreed we would fly as long as we had gas and the engine would run. I put a cord on my one-cell flashlight and hung it around my neck. I took off all my clothes except my shorts, socks and helmet. I loaded my .38 revolver with all tracers and put my shoulder holster on bare skin. The little flashlight or a tracer could be a life saver in the black water at night.

"All of our planes stayed with us in near radio silence. We flew directly to the Big E. She was landing planes and the lights were on. We made a standard squadron breakup and entered the landing pattern. About this time there was a bad crash on the *Enterprise's* deck. The skipper called and advised our squadron of the problem and told them to land on any base.

"Our radar was still on and all the ships appeared clearly. If they were carriers, I could even see if there were planes in their landing pattern. We picked a big one about two miles away and went over to land. There was no one in her pattern and we entered. As we slowed to approach attitude in our SBD, the big radial engine blocked most all of the skipper's forward view. He pulled down his goggles, opened the canopy and stuck his head way out to the port side. As he did this, everything went dark. He had dark-colored lens goggles. In his efforts to get everyone briefed and started this day, he forgot to change to clear lenses. The skipper asked me to help so I read the LSO signals; he made a perfect approach and we got the cut. As the power came off, we started a beautiful three-point drop and I thought we were falling into a black hole. The deck was so big it seemed to me we had to fall three times normal to get down to it. We had landed on the new *Yorktown*."

It was an extremely close call. Ramage's VB-10 pilots averaged four gallons remaining--perhaps five minutes flight time. Fellow SBD skipper Ralph Weymouth's squadron fared somewhat better, as VB-16 returnees had roughly 20 gallons in their final tank.

Undeniably, the aged Dauntless far outperformed the newer, trouble-plagued Helldiver. With one loss to fighters and three operationally, the SBDs sustained a 15 percent loss rate among the 27 launched. It was all the more amazing considering they flew more than half the mission--the entire outbound leg--carrying external ordnance which increased drag and, therefore, fuel consumption. A few days after the battle, Ramage tried to convince Vice Adm. Mitscher to "re-replace" SB2Cs with SBDs, but the Douglas production line was due to close in three weeks. Insufficient replacement parts and aircraft remained in the pipeline.

While the big, promising Helldiver had attained numerical superiority over the SBD, the Curtiss showed a clear deficiency. Both numerically and proportionally its combat and operational casualties were far greater than the Douglas: 15 percent losses to enemy defenses and 70 percent to fuel exhaustion or crashes. The 43 SB2Cs lost from the 51 launched represented the greatest single-mission casualty among U.S. Navy aircraft in World War Two--greater even than the three TBD squadrons destroyed at Midway. However, "The Beast" already was the focus of intense upgrading, and would finish the war with a creditable record thanks to unceasing efforts by aircrews and maintenance men.

As *Cavalla* and *Albacore* proved the day before, U.S. Navy torpedoes had become reliable and effective after two and one half years of war. Over the Mobile Fleet torpedo armed Avengers — less than ten per cent of the strike force — sank one hundred per cent of the combatant tonnage. Had another dozen TBFs carried their proper weapons, Ozawa might have lost another carrier that evening.

Missing with the ditched or shot-down aircraft were 78 pilots and 94 aircrewmen, plus six carrier sailors killed in flight-deck crashes. However, TF58's superb search-and-rescue effort eventually recovered three-quarters of the missing men: all but 17 pilots and 17 aircrew. Of the 138 fliers rescued, 85% were picked up by vigilant "smallboys"--the hard-working destroyers.

Wings folded, a Curtiss SB2C-1C Helldiver of VB-8 is manhandled onto an elevator on *Bunker Hill*. The forty-three Helldivers lost out of fifty-one launched on 20 June was a heavy price to pay for the sinking of one Japanese aircraft carrier and two oilers. (Author's coll. via R. M. Hill)

EPILOGUE

The First Battle of the Philippine Sea was only the world's fifth aircraft carrier duel, and not surprisingly it set historic precedents. It was the largest flattop engagement in history, and the only time in the 20th century that two future presidents were involved in the same battle: George Bush in *San Jacinto* and Gerald Ford in *Monterey*.

Another CVL officer was Lt. Cdr. Fred Bardshar of *Princeton's* VF-27, who rose to command TF77 during the Vietnam War and retired as a vice admiral. But 33 years after the Turkey Shoot he placed the events of 19 June 1944 in perspective: "There are two factors in our success. First, the training system in naval aviation was up to the challenge. It was able to produce aviators in the course of the war adequately trained for their mission. The Japanese were not: once their regulars were gone, their effectiveness fell off sharply and disastrously.

"Second, the F6F and its support was superb. It was rugged, forgiving and available. The availability was a combination of design, material support and maintenance know-how. This know-how was epitomized by VF-27's leading chief, ACCM Kenneth Colby, and his crew who routinely worked 20-hour days while on the line. The role of Colby and people like him should be acknowledged in any F6F story."

Concluded Samuel Eliot Morison: "Above all, the skill, initiative and intrepid courage of the young Hellcat pilots made this day one of the high points in the history of the American spirit."

LESSONS FOR TODAY

Despite the immense differences in ships and aircraft, a sailor or aviator transported from one of today's nuclear-powered carriers would have little trouble adjusting to procedures aboard a WW II carrier. In fact, the Philippine Sea battle contained

D3A2 Val which sought refuge on the island of Guam. This aircraft, 321-226, was one of seven which landed on Guam during the first day's battle. It was attached to the 321 Hikokitai of the 652nd Kokutai on board the carrier *Junyo*. (National Archives via J.F. Lansdale)

elements of every naval aviation community in existence today, with the exception of helicopters and airborne early warning planes.

In large part, the Marianas battle was a basis for what carrier air wings of the 1980s expected in a major war at sea against the Soviet Union. Ironically, the major differences were reversed: the Red Navy never fielded a genuine carrier threat while Japan's land-based aviation of the 1940s was far less capable than Russia's four decades later. However, four months after the Marianas battle, Japan launched "cruise missiles" against American warships, with increasing effectiveness. Controlled by a supremely adaptable guidance system, the *kamikaze* was immune to all electronic deception measures.

However, in June 1944 the similarities far outweighed the differences. Fleet air defense lay in the hands of Grumman fighters powered by Pratt-and-Whitney engines, while modifications to those planes also provided photographic reconnaissance. A tightly-woven electronic web permitted long-range detection and identification of hostile aircraft, which were then directed by ship-based controllers to intercept and destroy the intruders.

A primitive form of electronic warfare was conducted by the Japanese in the form of chaff. The effort proved ineffective, but did acknowledge the increasing importance of electronic countermeasures in naval warfare. A half-century later, each aircraft carrier has a small squadron dedicated specifically to that purpose.

In 1944 the greatest limiting factor of strike aircraft was range. In 1994 nothing has changed. Naval aviation remains locked in a controversy over its power-projection capability as the Grumman A-6 Intruder nears the end of its life. The F/A-18 Hornet strike-fighter is expected to fill the gap until a new deep-strike attack aircraft is designed, tested and produced. Retired WW II aviators share a sympathy with today's aviators who may yet be tethered to the 300-mile leash of the Mobile Fleet on 20 June 1944.

In aviation ordnance, antiship torpedoes no longer exist, and no American submarine has sunk a ship since 1945. Though cruise missiles have proven effective against stationary targets ashore, most war-at-sea scenarios still require a combination of "overhead" and "standoff" tactics with conventional and smart weapons. In other words, attack aviators still must fly in harm's way.

Despite the technical and quantitative superiority enjoyed by TF58, the decisive factors were leadership and training. At the squadron and air group/air wing levels, there is probably little to choose between then and now. After half a century, the high quality of professionalism found, for instance, in USS *Enterprise* (CV-6) doubtless is reflected in her nuclear-powered namesake (CVN-65). But with an evolving culture, standards change in five decades--and many aviators would say they have declined. The WW II generation was blessed with superior leadership, from Admirals King in Washington to Nimitz at CinCPac to Spruance at Fifth Fleet to Mitscher with TF58. One searches in vain for their counterparts a half-century later.

"Jig Dog" Ramage, skipper of Bombing Ten, became an air group commander late in the Korean War and served as a CarDiv chief of staff during Vietnam. Retired as a rear admiral, he reflected on his combat experience and how it effected him later in life:

"I know that without the wars that my max potential was lieutenant commander. I'm afraid that other warriors also would never have made (flag rank) under present policy. Performance in the Pentagon E-ring and political correctness are what counts. Today we have the best equipment and pilots in the world, but without strong leadership we will atrophy. The Tailhook 'scandal' is the best example. Loyalty down is a forgotten habit. I have waited in vain for any flag officer to say 'Enough!' Watching your six is good advice in the air, but it can be overdone when it comes to taking care of your most precious commodity--your people."

Of necessity, training is far more rigorous today. Aircrews now fly supersonic aircraft to demanding tolerances, day and night, with much greater safety than their axial-deck ancestors. However, current aviators probably never will log as many monthly hours as their WW II counterparts, for whom 15 hours per month would not only be insuffient--it would not even be much fun.

However, because of the success of naval aviators half a century ago, their children and grandchildren no longer contemplate another Battle of the Philippine Sea.

A6M5 Model 52 Zero in front of hangar on Saipan airfield No. 1 (also known as Aslito Airfield). 61-120 was assigned to fighter Hikotai S.1 attached to 261st Kokutai. It was one of over twenty captured on the field. Many were returned to the U.S. for testing and as war trophies. Today G1-120 is the sole example of a Zero flying with the original engine. It is also the centerpiece of the Ed Maloney Collection at the Chino Air Museum. (J.F. Lansdale)

A6M3 Model 22 belonging to 261st Kokutai Tora ("Tiger") Unit. Rope webbing was used to attach vegetation for ground camouflage. Kanji symbol for "Tora" was later replaced by the numeral 61. (National Archives via J.F. Lansdale)

A6M5 Zero of fighter Hikotai S.8 attached to the newly formed 265th Kokutai. This unit was decimated within hours of landing on Saipan. Kanji symbol on 8-17 is "Gun" . The symbol may have constituted a portion of the pilot's name, however it is more likely the name of the aircraft. The symbol means "Army" or "Troops". (Juzo Nakamura via J.F. Lansdale)

A6M5 attached to Hikotai S.8 of the 265th Kokutai. Kanji symbol on 8-34 represents the word for "Woods" or "Forest". (Juzo Nakamura via J.F. Lansdale)

USN ORDER OF BATTLE

TASK FORCE 58 ORGANIZATION
As of 13 June 1944
CTF 58 Vice Adm. Marc Mitscher
Task Group 58.1 Rear Adm. J.J. Clark

USS Yorktown (CV–10)
Capt. R.E. Jennings
Air Group 1: Cdr. J.M. Pete

VF–1	42	F6F–3	Cdr. B.M. Strean
VB–1	40	SB2C–1C	LCdr. J.W. Runyan
VT–1	17	TBF/TBM–1C	LCdr. W.F. Henry
VFN–77 Det B	5	F6F–3N	Lt. A.C. Benjes

USS Hornet (CV–12)
Capt. W.D. Sample
Air Group 2: Cdr. J.D. Arnold

VF–2	37	F6F–3	Cdr. W.A. Dean Jr.
VB–2	33	SB2C–1C	LCdr. G.B. Campbell
VT–2	18	TBF/TBM–1C	LCdr. L.M.D. Ford
VFN–76 Det B	4	F6F–3N	Lt. R.L. Reiserer

USS Belleau Wood (CVL–24)
Capt. J. Perry
Air Group 24: LCdr. E.M. Link

VF–24	24	F6F–3	LCdr. Link
VT–24	9	TBF/TBM–1C	Lt. R.M. Swensson

USS Bataan (CVL–29)
Capt. V.H. Schaeffer
Air Group 50: LCdr. J.C. Strange

VF–50	24	F6F–3	LCdr. Strange
VT–50	9	TBF/TBM–1C	LCdr. L.K. Swanson

Task Group 58.2 Rear Adm. A.E. Montgomery

USS Bunker Hill (CV–17)
Capt. T.P. Jeter
Air Group 8: Cdr. R.L. Shifley

VF–8	38	F6F–3	Cdr. W.M. Collins
VB–8	33	SB2C–1	LCdr. J.D. Arbes
VT–8	18	TBF/TBM–1C	Cdr. K.F. Musick
VFN–76 Det A	4	F6F–3N	LCdr. E.P. Aurand

USS Wasp (CV–14)
Capt. C.A.F. Sprague
Air Group 14: Cdr. W.C. Wingard

VF–14	35	F6F–3	LCdr. E.W. Biros
VB–14	32	SB2C–1C	LCdr. J.D. Blitch
VT–14	18	TBF–1C/D	LCdr. H.S. Roberts
VFN–77 Det C	6	F6F–3N	Lt. J.H. Boyum

USS Monterey (CVL–26)
Capt. S.H. Ingersoll
Air Group 28: LCdr. R.W. Mehle

VF–28	21	F6F–3	LCdr. Mehle
VT–28	8	TBM–1C	Lt. R.P. Gift

USS Cabot (CVL–28)
Capt. S.J. Michael
Air Group 31: Cdr. R.A. Winston

VF–31	24	F6F–3	Cdr. Winston
VT–31	9	TBF/TBM–1C	Lt. E.E. Wood

Task Group 58.3 Rear Adm. J.W. Reeves

USS Enterprise (CV–6)
Capt. M.B. Gardner
Air Group 10: Cdr. W.R. Kane

VF–10	31	F6F–3	Lt. R.W. Schuman
VB–10	21	SBD–5	LCdr. J.D. Ramage
VT–10	14	TBF/TBM–1C	LCdr. W.I. Martin
VFN–101 Det A	3	F4U–2	LCdr. R.E. Harmer

USS Lexington (CV–16)
Capt. E.W. Litch
Air Group 16: Cdr. E.M. Snowden

VF–16	38	F6F–3	Cdr. P.B. Buie
VB–16	34	SBD–5	LCdr. R.A. Weymouth
VT–16	18	TBF/TBM–1C	Lt. N.A. Sterrie
VFN–76 Det C	4	F6F–3N	Lt. W.H. Abercrombie

USS Princeton (CVL–23)
Capt. W.H. Buracker
Air Group 27: LCdr. E.W. Wood (KIA)

VF–27	24	F6F–3	LCdr. Wood
VT–27	9	TBM–1C	LCdr. S.M. Haley

USS San Jacinto (CVL–30)
Capt. H.M. Martin
Air Group 51: Cdr. C.L. Moore

VF–51	24	F6F–3	Cdr. Moore
VT–51	9	TBM–1C	LCdr. D.J. Melvin

Task Group 58.4 Rear Adm. W. K. Harrill

USS Essex (CV–9)
Capt. R.A. Oftsie
Air Group 15: Cdr. D. McCampbell

VF–15	39	F6F–3	LCdr. C.W. Brewer
VB–15	36	SB2C–1C	LCdr. J.H. Mini
VT–15	20	TBF/TBM–1C	LCdr. V.G. Lambert
VFN–77 Det A	4	F6F–3N	Lt. R.M. Freeman

USS Cowpens (CVL–25)
Capt. W.H. Taylor
Air Group 25: LCdr. R.H. Price

VF–25	26	F6F–3	LCdr. Price
VT–25	9	TBF/TBM–1C	Lt. R.B. Cunningham

USS Langley (CVL–27)
Capt. W.M. Dillon
Air Group 32: Cdr. E.C. Outlaw

VF–32	25	F6F–3	Cdr. Outlaw
VT–32	9	TBF/TBM–1C	Lt. D.A. Marks

Task Group 58.7 Vice Adm. W.A. Lee
Battleship support force

Summary of TF58 Aircraft

F6F–3	452
F6F–3N	27
F4U–2	3
SB2C–1	174
SBD–5	55
TBF/TBM–1	194
Total	905

Task Group 58.3 (cont.)

ESCORT CARRIER SUPPORT FORCE
As of 13 June 1944
Task Group 52.11 Rear Adm. H.B. Sallada

USS Kitkun Bay (CVE–71)
Capt. J.P. Whitney
VC–5 Lt. Cdr. R.L. Fowler 12 FM–2, 8 TBM–1C

USS Gambier Bay (CVE–73)
Capt. H.H. Goodwin
VC–10 Lt. Cdr. E.H. Huxtable 12 FM–2, 9 TBM–1C

USS Coral Sea (CVE–57)
Capt. W. Watson
VC–33 Lt. Cdr. R. Gray   14 FM–2, 12 TBF/TBM–1C

USS Corregidor (CVE–58)
Capt. R.L. Thomas
VC–41 Lt. Cdr. A.P. Kolonie 14 FM–2, 12 TBM–1C

Task Group 52.14 Rear Adm. G.E. Bogan

USS Kalinin Bay (CVE–68)
Capt. C.R. Brown
VC–3 Lt. Cdr. W.H. Keighley   14 FM–2, 9 TBM–1C

USS White Plains (CVE–66)
Capt. O.A. Weller
VC–4 Lt. E.R. Fickenscher   16 FM–2, 12 TBF/TBM–1C

USS Midway (CVE–63)
Capt. F.J. McKenna
VC–65 Lt. Cdr. R.M. Jones 12 FM–2, 9 TBM–1C

USS Fanshaw Bay (CVE–70)
Capt. D.P. Johnson
VC–68 Lt. Cdr. R.S. Rogers 16 FM–2, 12 TBM–1C

110 FM–2
83 TBF/TBM–1C
193 CVE aircraft

PATROL PLANES BASED OFF SAIPAN

USS Ballard (AVD–10)
Cdr. G.C. Nichandross
VP–16 Lt. Cdr. W.J. Scarpino 5 PBM–5

ESCORT CARRIER REINFORCEMENT FORCE

USS Manila Bay (CVE–61)
318th Fighter Group: Lt. Col. L. Sanders
73rd F.S. P–47D   Major J. Hussey

USS Natoma Bay (CVE–62)
19th F.S. P–47D   Major H. McAfee

USS Sargent Bay (CVE–83)
333rd F.S. P–47D   Major P. Fojtik
Approximately 78 aircraft

JAPANESE ORDER OF BATTLE

FIRST TASK FLEET ORGANIZATION
As of 13 June 1944

Commander–in–Chief: Vice Adm. Jisaburo Ozawa
Carrier Division One: Vice Adm. Ozawa
HMIJS Taiho
Capt. Tomozo Kikuchi
Hikotai 311
HMIJS Shokaku
Capt. Hiroshi Sugihara
Hikotai 312
HMIJS Zuikaku
Capt. Takeo Kaizuka
Hikotai 313
Air Group 601: Cdr. Toshiie Irisa
Attack leader: Lt. Cdr. Akira Taru
Fighter squadrons: Lt. Yasuo Masuyama
Bomber squadrons: Lt. Cdr. Kenji Ono
Torpedo squadrons: Lt. Cdr. Tarui
Scouting units: unknown

A6M5, Model 52	80
A6M2, Model 21	11
B6N1	44
D4Y1 (incl. recon models)	70
D3A2	9

Carrier Division Two: Rear Adm. Takaji Joshima
HMIJS Junyo
Capt. Kiyomi Shibuya
Hikotai 321
HMIJS Hiyo
Capt. Toshiyuki Yokoi (KIA)
Hikotai 322
HMIJS Ryuho
Capt. Tokio Kamei
Hikotai 323
Air Group 652: Cdr. Shoichi Suzuki
Attack leader: Lt. Cdr. Jozo Iwami
Fighter squadrons: Lt. Yasuhei Kobayashi
Fighter–bombers: Lt. Hiroshi Yoshimura
Bomber squadrons: Lt. Zenji Abe
Torpedo squadrons: Lt. Cdr. Iwami

A6M5, Model 52	53
A6M2, Model 21	27
B6N1	15
D4Y1	11
D3A2	29

Carrier Division Three: Rear Adm. Sueo Obayashi
HMIJS Chitose
Capt. Yoshiyuki Kishi
Hikotai 331
HMIJS Chiyoda
Capt. Eichiro Joh
Hikotai 332
HMIJS Zuiho
Capt. Takuro Sugiura
HIkotai 333
Air Group 653: Cdr. Gunji Kumura
Attack leader: Lt. Cdr. Masauyki Yamagami
Fighter squadrons: Toshi Taka Ito
Fighter–bombers: Kenji Nakagawa
Torpedo squadrons: Lt. Cdr. Yamagami

A6M5, Model 52	17
A6M2, Model 21	46
B6N1	9
B5N2	18

JAPANESE ORDER OF BATTLE (cont.)

A6M5 fighter	150
A6M2 fighter–bomber	84
D3A2 dive bomber	38
D4Y1 dive bomber, scout	81
B5N2 torpedo plane	18
B6N1 torpedo plane	68
Actual carrier a/c embarked	439

BASE AIR FORCE
Vice Adm. Kakuji Kakuta
61st Air Flotilla: Rear Adm Ueno

Air Group 121: Cdr. Iwao
Tinian Hikotai T.1 C6N1 10
Palau Hikotai T.2 D4Y1 10
Air Group 261: Cdr. Ueda
Saipan Hikotai S.1, S.2 A6M5 80
Air Group 263: Cdr. Tamai
Guam Hikotai S.3, S.4 A6M5 80
Air Group 265: Cdr. Urata
Guam Hikotai S.7, S.8 A6M5 80
Air Group 321: Cdr. Kubo
Tinian Hikotai S.801, S.802 J1N 30
Air Group 343: Cdr. Takenaka
Palau Hikotai S.403 A6M5 40
Air Group 521: Cdr. Kamei
Guam Hikotai K.401 P1Y 40
Tinian Hikotai K.402 P1Y 40
Air Group 523: Cdr. Wada
Tinian Hikotai K.1,K.2 D4Y1 40
Air Group 761: Cdr. Matsumoto
Tinian Hikotai K. 601 G4M2 40
Palau Hikotai K.602 G4M2 40
Air Group 1021: Cdr. Kurihara
Tinian Hikotai U.1, U.2 L2D 20
22nd Air Flotilla: Rear Adm. Sumikawa
Air Group 755: Cdr. Kusumoto
Guam Hikotai K.701 G4M2 40
Truk Hikotai K.702 G4M2 40

A6M5 fighter	280
C6N1 reconnaissance	10
D4Y1 dive bomber, recon	50
G4M2 twin-engined bomber	160
J1N twin-engined night fighter	30
L2D twin-engined transport	20
P1Y twin-engined bomber	80
Total	630*

* These are authorized strengths; actual probably was less.

Note: The proper identification of Japanese naval and air units for this work has been intensive. We have used the term Kokutai for the air groups and Hikotai for the subordinate squadrons. Those Japanese squadrons aboard carriers were actually "Hikokitai" – airplane units – while land based units were referred to as "Hikotai", meaning, air units. To avoid confusion we have taken the liberty of using only the Hikotai term.

It will also be noted that Japanese shore based squadrons bore a number such as "S.2". This meant Sentoki (the Japanese word for fighter) Hikotai 2. Similarly Kogeki, attack (bomber) units were K.,Teisatsu, recon units, carried a T, and Unso units were transport with a U.

KEY JAPANESE FIGHTER PILOT LOSSES

NAME	RANK	UNIT SQ/GRP	DATE
Ikuro Sakami	Lt.	/601	19 Jun 44
Kiyoshi Fukagawa	Lt.	/601	19 Jun 44
Toshida Kawazoc	Lt.	/601	19 Jun 44
Mamoru Morita	CPO	/601	19 Jun 44
Akira Maruyama	Ens.	/601	19 Jun 44
Ichiro Yamamoto	WO	/601	19 Jun 44
Masayuki Hanamura	CPO	/601	19 Jun 44
Saburo Sugai	WO	/601	19 Jun 44
Shun-ichi Koyanagi	CPO	/601	19 Jun 44
Hiroshi Yoshimura	Lt.	/652	19 Jun 44
Kenkichi Takasawa	Lt.	/652	19 Jun 44
Yoshihiko Takenaka	WO	/652	19 Jun 44
Kenta Komiyama	WO	/652	19 Jun 44
Ko-ichi Imamura	CPO	/652	19 Jun 44
Hiroshi Shiozaka	Lt.	/653	19 Jun 44
Kiyotaka Sawazaki	PO1c	/653	19 Jun 44
Isao Kondo	CPO	/653	19 Jun 44
Kozaburo Yasui	WO	/652	19 Jun 44
Masami Komaru	CPO	/652	19 Jun 44
Tetsuo Kikuchi	CPO	/652	19 Jun 44
Fumio Yamagata	Lt.	/601	19 Jun 44
Yutaka Yagi	Lt.	/601	19 Jun 44
Toshio Fukushima	Lt.	/601	19 Jun 44
Fumio Ito	CPO	/601	19 Jun 44
Mitsunobu Kaga	Lt(jg)	/601	19 Jun 44
Iwao Yamamoto	CPO	/601	19 Jun 44
Susumu Hoiro	Lt.	/601	19 Jun 44
Takeo Nagai	CPO	/601	19 Jun 44
Shinya Ozaki	Lt.	/343	19 Jun 44
Isao Doikawa	CPO	/343	19 Jun 44
Kiyoshi Yoshioka	PO1c	/343	19 Jun 44
Tatsuo Hirano	Lt.	309/	19 Jun 44
Yoshinao Tokuji	WO	/253	19 Jun 44
Noboru Kayahara	CPO	/253	19 Jun 44
Ko-ichi Yamauchi	CPO	/201	19 Jun 44
Naoto Sato	CPO	/261	19 Jun 44
Shigenori Hayashi	CPO	/261	19 Jun 44
Takumi Kai	WO	/652	20 Jun 44
Jiro Imura	WO	/652	20 Jun 44
Masahiro Motoki	CPO	/652	20 Jun 44

Data on Key Japanese Fighter Pilot Losses was extracted from **Japanese Naval Aces and Fighter Units in World War II** by Ikuhiko Hata and Yasuho Izawa, translated by Don C. Gorham, published in 1989 by Naval Institute Press, Appendix B. We are indebted to the Naval Institute Press for their permission to reproduce.

Estimated Japanese aircraft losses to all causes:

19 Jun 44	342
20 Jun 44	65
Total	407

VF–1, USS YORKTOWN

Lt(jg) C.H. Ambellan	3 Zekes
Lt. R.R. Baysinger	1 Zeke
Lt(jg) R.A. Bechtol	1 Zeke, 1 Tony
Lt. L.F. Clark	2 Jakes
Lt(jg) R.T. Eastmond	3 Zekes, 1 Tony
Lt(jg) R.A. Frink	2 Zekes, 1 Tony
Lt(jg) J.F. Hankins	2 Tony, 1 Zeke
Ens. R.W. Matz	1 Zeke, 1 Tony
Lt. W.C. Moseley	2 Zekes
Lt. H.J. Mueller	1 Zeke
Cdr. J.M. Peters (CAG)	2 Zekes
Ens J.R. Pfister	1 Zeke, 1 Kate
Lt. R.H. Shireman Jr.	1 Zeke
Lt(jg) G.W. Staeheli	1 Tony
Cdr. B.M. Strean (CO)	1 Zeke, 1 Tony
Lt(jg) M.M. Tomme Jr.	1 Zeke, 1 Tony
Lt(jg) W.P. Tukey	2 Zekes
Lt(jg) B.Y. Weber	1 Zeke
Ens W.F. Wolf	1 Zeke
19 pilots	**37 victories**

VF–10, USS ENTERPRISE

Lt. R.O. Devine	2 Zekes, 1 Judy, 1 Val
Ens. C.D. Farmer	1 Kate
Lt. D. Gordon	1 Judy
Lt(jg) R.F. Kanze	2 Vals
Lt(jg) J.F. Kay	1 Val, 2 Zekes
Lt(jg) P.L. Kirkwood	1 Judy, 1 Val, 1 Kate
Lt(jg) M.P. Long Jr.	2 Zekes
Lt(jg) R.W. Maston	1 Judy
Lt(jg) V.R. Ude	1 Nate, 1 Zeke, 1 Kate
9 pilots	**20 victories**

VF–14, USS WASP

Ens. P.A. Coari	.5 Betty
Ens. J.H. Dougherty	1 Zeke
Ens. D.W. Fisher	.5 Zeke
Ens. C.M. Houston	1 Zeke
Lt. W.M. Knight	1 Kate, .5 Tony
Lt(jg) M.R. Novak	1.5 Tonys
Lt. W.Q. Punnel	1 Zeke
Ens. W.E. Schmidt	1 Jill
Ens. E.J. Streeter	.5 Zeke
Lt. E.B. Turner	1 Zeke
Lt. F.E. Standring	1 Zeke
Lt(jg) R.L. Straub	1 Zeke
12 pilots	**11.5 victories**

VF–2, USS HORNET

Lt. W.K. Blair	2 Vals
Lt(jg) C.L. Carlson	1 Zeke
Lt(jg) D.A. Carmichael	2 Jills, 1 Zeke
Lt. C.H. Carroll	2 Vals
Ens. A.D. Connard	1 Zeke
Cdr. W.A. Dean (CO)	2 Zekes
Ens. P.A. Doherty	2 Zekes
Lt. R.J. Griffin	2 Zekes
Lt(jg) R.H. Grimes Jr.	1 Zeke
Lt(jg) N. Harrigan Jr.	1 Jill
Lt. Cdr. L.E. Harris	1 Zeke
Ens. K.B. Lake	1 Val
Lt(jg) M.E. Noble	1 Zeke
Lt(jg) J.J. O'Brien	1 Zeke
Lt(jg) D.R. Park	1 Zeke
Lt(jg) E.D. Redmond	2 Zekes
Ens. L.R. Robinson	2 Zekes
Lt(jg) W.A. Skon	2 Vals
Lt. A. Van Haren	2 Zekes
Ens. W.H. Vaughan Jr.	3 Zekes
Lt(jg) M.W. Vineyard	1 Zeke
Lt. R.M. Voris	1 Zeke
Ens. W.B. Webb	6 Vals
Lt(jg) J.T. Wolf	1 Zeke
Lt(jg) E.W. Zaeske	1 Zeke
25 pilots	**43 victories**

VF–15, USS ESSEX

Ens. J.D. Bare	1 Jake, 1 Kate
Ens. N.R. Berree	2 Hamps, 1 Judy
Cdr. C.W. Brewer (CO)	3 Zekes, 2 Judys
Lt(jg) G.R. Carr	5 Judys
Lt. J.J. Collins	1 Zeke
Ens. J.E. Duffy	1 Zeke
Lt. Cdr. G.C. Duncan	3 Zekes
Ens. R.E. Foltz	2 Judys
Ens. R.E. Fowler Jr.	3 Zekes, 1 Hamp
Ens. L.S. Hamblin	1 Zeke
Lt(jg) W.V. Henning	1.5 Zekes
Ens. D.E. Johnson Jr.	1 Val
Ens. W.R. Johnson	1 Zeke
Lt.(jg) W.A. Lundin	1 Zeke, 1 Judy
Cdr. D. McCampbell (CAG)	5 Judys, 2 Zekes
Ens. G.E. Mellon Jr.	1 Judy, 1 Zeke
Lt(jg) C.B. Milton	2 Zekes
Ens. R.L. Nall	1 Zeke
Lt. E.W. Overton Jr.	1 Judy, 3 Zekes
Ens. G.W. Pigman Jr.	3 Judys
Ens. C.W. Plant	4 Zekes
Ens. J.W. Power Jr.	2 Zekes
Lt. Cdr. J.F. Rigg	1 Val
Lt. J.R. Strane	1 Judy, 1 Jake, 1 Jill
Lt(jg) J.C.C. Symmes	1.5 Zekes, 1 Judy
Ens. T. Tarr	1 Zeke
Ens. T.E. Thompson	1 Zeke
Ens. W.V. Twelves	2 Zekes
Lt(jg) C. White	.5 Zeke
29 pilots	**68.5 victories**

VF–8, USS BUNKER HILL

Lt(jg) C.H. Allan	1 Zeke
Lt(jg) T.I. Brown Jr.	1 Zeke
Lt(jg) H.T. Brownscombe	2 Zekes
Lt(jg) J.B. Czerny	1 Zeke
Lt(jg) E.J. Dooner	1 Zeke
Lt. H.I. Gustafson	1 Zeke
Lt(jg) L.P. Heinzen	1 Zeke, 1 Topsy
Lt. Cdr. R.W. Hoel	1 Zeke, 1 Judy
Lt(jg) G.N. Kirk	1 Zeke
Lt(jg) W.E. Lamoreaux	1 Jake
Lt. Cdr. E.S. McCuskey	1 Zeke
Lt(jg) T.P. O'Boyle	1 Zeke
Lt(jg) J.W. Topliff	1 Zeke, 1 Hamp
Lt(jg) J.D. Vanderhoof	3 Hamp
14 pilots	**20 victories**

VF–50, USS BATAAN

Lt. L.W. Abbott Jr.	1 Judy
Ens. W.A. McCormick	2 Judys
Ens. C.G. Miller	1 Zeke
Lt(jg) D.R. Rehm Jr.	3 Zekes
Ens. F.V. Smith	1 Jake
Ens. E.R. Tarleton	1 Judy, 1 Jill
Lt(jg) P.C. Thomas	1 Zeke
7 pilots	**11 victories**

VB–14, USS WASP

Lt. Cdr. A.L. Downing's flight	1 Judy
Ens. C.J. Haggerty	.5 Betty
7 pilots	**1.5 victories**

VF–32, USS LANGLEY

Ens. S. Bienvenu	1 Judy
Lt(jg) J.D. Keyser	1 Zeke
2 pilots	**2 victories**

VB–15, USS ESSEX

Lt(jg) C. Jordan	1 Kate
1 pilot	**1 victory**

VF(N)–76, USS HORNET

Lt.Cdr. E.P. Aurand (CO)	1 Jill
Lt(jg) F.R. Dungan	1 Kate, 1 Zeke
Ens. W.E. Levering	1 Val
Lt. R.R. Reiserer	5 Vals
4 pilots	**9 victories**

VF–16, USS LEXINGTON

Ens. W.H. Albert	2 Jills
Lt(jg) J.W. Bartol	2 Jills
Lt(jg) W.R. Bauhof	1 Jill, 1 Zeke, 2 Judys
Ens. H.W. Brockmeyer	1 Zeke, 1 Judy
Ens. J.S. Christiansen	1 Kate
Lt(jg) A.H. Durham Jr.	1 Zeke
Lt(jg) A.R. Fizalkowski	1 Judy
Lt(jg) F.M. Fleming	2 Jills
Lt(jg) A.L. Frendberg	1 Zeke
Ens. R.F. Frey	1 Zeke
Ens. B.F. Hagie	3 Zekes
Lt(jg) E.R. Hanks	1 Zeke
Ens. H.R. Gentry	1 Judy
Lt. E.A. Kraft	1 Zeke
Lt(jg) A.V. McPhillips Jr.	1 Kate, 3 Zekes
Lt(jg) Z.W. Neff	1 Jill, 2 Zekes, 1 Jake
Lt(jg) R.M. Pound Jr.	1 Judy
Ens. E.R. Ross	1 Jake, 1 VT
Ens. D.E. Satterfield	1 Zeke
Ens. W.J. Seyfferle	1 Zeke
Lt(jg) G.K. Sherman	1 Jake, 1 Jill
Cdr. E.M. Snowden	1 Judy
Lt(jg) A. Vraciu	6 Judys
Ens. E.H. Wendorf	1 bomber
24 pilots	46 victories

VF–28, USS MONTEREY

Lt. O.C. Bailey	4 Zekes
Ens. G.J. Barnes	2 Jills
Lt. D.C. Clements	3 Zekes
Lt. W.A. Dryer	.5 Jill
Lt(jg) W.T. Fitzpatrick	.5 Judy
Ens. R.P. Granger	.5 Judy, .5 Jill
Lt. D.W. Koster	.5 Jill
Lt. Cdr. R.W. Mehle (CO)	2 Jills
Ens. J.C. Parsons	1 Zeke
Ens. A.C. Persson	1 Zeke
Ens. W.G. Shackelford	.5 Jill
Ens. R.P. Sherrai	2 Zekes
Lt. R.G. Thorpe	1 Zeke
13 pilots	19 victories

VT–16, USS LEXINGTON

Ens. E.P. Baker	1 Zeke
Lt(jg) H.C. Thomas	1 Zeke
2 pilots	2 victories

VF–25, USS COWPENS

Lt(jg) M.L. Adams	1 Zeke
Lt. Cdr. G.B. Brown	1.5 Zekes
Ens. E.W. Haley	1 Zeke
Lt. H.J. Kicker	1 Jill
Lt(jg) D.J. McKinley	2 Jills
Ens. J.I. Nourse	2 Jills
Lt(jg) R.I. Raffman	.5 Zeke
7 pilots	9 victories

VF–31, USS CABOT

Ens. W.G. Andrews	1 Zeke
Lt(jg) J.M. Bowie	1 Zeke
Lt(jg) R.D. Conant	1 Zeke
Ens. C.W. Dietrich	1 Zeke
Lt(jg) D.B.J. Driscoll	1 Zeke
Lt(jg) D.B. Galt Jr.	1 Zeke
Ens. S.W. Godsey	1 Judy
Lt(jg) A.R. Hawkins	3 Zekes
Lt(jg) F.R. Hayde	3 Zekes
Lt. S.G. Kona	1 Zeke
Lt.D.W. Mulcahy	2 Zekes
Lt(jg) H.H. Scales	1 Zeke, 1 Judy
Lt. J.S. Stewart	3 Zekes
Lt. C.H. Turner	3 Zekes
Lt(jg) J.L. Wirth	4 Zekes
15 pilots	28 victories

VC–10, USS GAMBIER BAY

Lt. W.R. Roby	.5 Kate
Ens. J.F. Lischer	.5 Kate
2 pilots	1 victory

206 F6F pilots credited with	371.5 victories
10 VB/VT pilots credited with	4.5 "
6 FM pilots credited with	4 "
222 TF–58/52 pilots	380 claims

VF–24, BELLEAU WOOD

Lt(jg) L.E. Graham	1 Zeke
Lt. E.R. Hardin Jr.	1 Zeke
Lt(jg) J.P. Herr	2 Zekes
Ens. E. Holmgaard	1 Zeke
Lt. C.I. Oveland	1 Zeke
Lt(jg) R.C. Tabler	1 Zeke
Lt(jg) R.H. Thelen	3 Zekes
7 pilots	10 victories

VF–27, USS PRINCETON

Lt. Cdr. F.A. Bardshar (CO)	2 Judys
Lt. H.F. Brotherton	2 Tonys
Lt. C.A. Brown Jr.	1 Tony
Ens. R.M. Burnell	2 Judys, 1 Tony
Ens. L.A. Erickson	1 Zeke, 1 Kate
Lt(jg) W.E. Lamb	1 Zeke, 3 Kates
Ens. H.D. Lillie	1 Zeke, 1 Kate
Lt(jg) H.F. Loveland	1 Zeke
Lt. J.L. McMahon	1 Tony
Ens. R.M. Russell	1 Zeke
Lt(jg) J.A. Shirley	2 Zekes
Lt. R.E. Stambook	3 Zekes, 1 Judy
Ens. G.A. Stanley	2 Zekes, 2 Tonys
Lt. R.S. Taylor	1 Zeke
14 pilots	30 victories

VF–51, USS SAN JACINTO

Lt(jg) R.F. Grant	1 Tony
Ens. W.H. Hile	1 Tony, 1 Judy
Lt(jg) H. Isherwood Jr.	1 Betty
Lt. W.R. Maxwell	1 Judy
Cdr. C.L. Moore Jr.(CO)	1.5 Tonys
Lt(jg) D.G. Stewart	1 Zeke
6 pilots	7.5 victories

VC–41, USS CORREGIDOR

Lt(jg) H.A. Caravacci	.5 Zeke
Lt. G.V. Knudson	.5 Zeke
Ens. F.N. Davis	1 Zeke
Lt(jg) J.F. Perry	1 Zeke
4 pilots	3 victories

TOP INDIVIDUAL SCORES, 19 JUNE

Pilot	Unit	Score	Wartime Total	Comments
Cdr. D. McCampbell	VF–15	5 Judys, 1 prob. 2 Zekes	34	2 sorties
Lt(jg) A. Vraciu	VF–16	6 Judys	19	
Ens. W.B. Webb	VF–2	6 Vals, 2 prob.	7	
Cdr. C.W. Brewer	VF–15	5 Zekes	6.5	2 sorties, KIA
Lt(jg) G.R. Carr	VF–15	5 Judys	11.5	
Lt. R.L. Reiserer	VF(N)–76	5 Vals	9	
		34 (av. 5.5)	87 (av. 14.5)	

TASK FORCE 58 LOSSES
JUNE 19

	Combat	Operational	Totals
F6F	13	5	18
VB/VT	6	6	12
	19	11	30

27 pilots and aircrew killed or missing, 31 ships' company killed.

JUNE 20

	Combat	Operational	Totals
F6F	7	14	21
SB2C	8	35 *	43
SBD	1	3	4
TBF	4	25	29
	20	77	97

34 pilots and aircrew killed or missing plus 2 on ships, 6 ships' company killed.

* Includes 2 SB2Cs jettisoned with battle damage.

BIBLIOGRAPHY

Buell, Harold L. **Dauntless Helldivers**. New York: Orion Books,1991.

Hata, Ikuhiko and Izawa, Yasuho, translated by Don C. Gorham. **Japanese Naval Aces and Fighter Units in World War II**, Annapolis, MD, Naval Institute Press, 1989.

Miller, Thomas G. "Anatomy of an Air Battle." AAHS Journal, Summer 1970.

Morison, Samuel E. **New Guinea and the Marianas**. Boston: Little, Brown, 1953.

Olynyk, Frank. USN Credits for Destruction of Enemy Aircraft, WW II. Aurora: privately printed, 1982

Polmar, Norman. **Aircraft Carriers**. Garden City: Doubleday, 1969.

Ramage, James D. "A Review of the Philippine Sea Battle." The Hook, August 1990.

Reynolds, Clark G. **The Fast Carriers.** New York: McGraw–Hill, 1968.

Rogers, Allen. J. "The View from TorpRon 28." The Hook, August 1990.

Shores, Christopher. **Duel for the Sky.** U.K.: Blandford Press, 1985.

Tillman, Barrett. Hellcat. Annapolis: Naval Institute Press, 1979.

—— **TBF–TBM Avenger at War**. U.K.: Ian Allan Ltd., 1979.

U.S. Navy. ACA–1 reports and war diaries for many of the squadrons engaged.

—— The Campaigns of the Pacific War. Washington, D.C.: Naval Analysis Division, 1946.

—— "History of Naval Fighter Direction." CIC Magazine, June 1946.

—— Location and Allowance of Navy Aircraft, 13 June 1944.

—— Naval Air Operations in the Marianas. Washington, D.C.

Wendorf, E.G. "More on the Marianas." American Fighter Aces Bulletin, Spring 1993.

Y'Blood, Tom. **Red Sun Setting**. Annapolis: Naval Institute Press, 1981.

—— **The Little Giants**. Annapolis: Naval Institute Press, 1988.